C0-AWH-653

250/10

CHRISTIANITY
AS
HISTORY AND FAITH

OTHER BOOKS BY
ARTHUR CUSHMAN McGIFFERT

———

A HISTORY OF CHRISTIAN THOUGHT
    Vol. I.   EARLY AND EASTERN
    Vol. II. THE WEST FROM TERTULLIAN TO
             ERASMUS
THE GOD OF THE EARLY CHRISTIANS
THE RISE OF MODERN RELIGIOUS IDEALS
MARTIN LUTHER, THE MAN AND HIS WORK
PROTESTANT THOUGHT BEFORE KANT
THE APOSTLES' CREED
A HISTORY OF CHRISTIANITY IN THE APOS-
    TOLIC AGE
THE CHURCH HISTORY OF EUSEBIUS
DIALOGUE BETWEEN A CHRISTIAN AND A JEW

CHRISTIANITY
AS
HISTORY AND FAITH

BY

ARTHUR CUSHMAN McGIFFERT

EDITED BY

A. C. McGIFFERT, Jr.

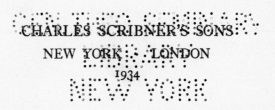

CHARLES SCRIBNER'S SONS

NEW YORK · LONDON

1934

270T
M174

99527

Copyright, 1934, by
CHARLES SCRIBNER'S SONS

Printed in the United States of America

*All rights reserved. No part of this book
may be reproduced in any form without
the permission of Charles Scribner's Sons*

A

TO
G. H. M.

PREFACE

This volume not only presents further illuminating studies in the history of Christianity, but supplements the ripe wisdom of the author's scholarship by a statement of his own living faith. He is known primarily as a scholar, one of the foremost authorities in the United States, in fact, on the history of Christianity. His books and articles, which won for him his reputation, exhibit but indirectly his own Christian faith and conscience. Yet like other leading scholars of liberal Christianity, he presents a combination of scientific and religious devotion as signal as that exhibited by outstanding men in any of the divisions of the Christian church at any period of its history. The contribution of these leaders is as significant in the realm of faith as in the realm of truth. Fearless and independent as their criticism may be, these modernists display no impoverishment or weakening of their confidence in the Christian gospel.

Part I is strictly historical and defines the issues and insights that separate the three main types of Christians, Roman Catholics, Protestants and Modernists. Part II represents the main structure of my father's personal religion, which motivated his research and formed the content of his preaching. Incomplete as the material is, it forms a self-consistent, historically and contemporaneously significant interpretation of the Christian religion in frank, forceful and appealing terms.

Although forced by ill-health to resign from Union Theological Seminary in 1926, my father did not relinquish the hope of continuing his researches. Among his manuscripts at the time of his death was a sheaf of papers on which he had jotted down the titles of several books he would like to write. "Three small books," reads one of these sheets, "Christianity Old and New; The Evolution of Christianity; What It Has Meant to Be a Christian; two large books, Early Church History [for which the chapter headings are worked out]; A History of Christian Thought." Others of these suggestive titles are: A Brief History of the Christian Religion; The Christian Heritage: from Judaism, Orientalism, Hellenism, Rome, the North; The Christian Religion, Its Rise and Persistence; Christian Origins: of the Church, the Sacraments, the Creed, the Canon, the Episcopate, the Papacy; The Christian Man, an Historical Study; Christianity in the Making (with six chapter headings). In addition he listed the titles of several projected articles and a volume of Collected Addresses on Christianity and Democracy.

As the first project from among this rich mass of possibilities he turned to the general history of Christian Thought. This grew under his hand, until the treatment of the course of thought from the beginning to the Protestant Reformation called for two volumes. Immediately after the publication of the second of these books in 1933 he began the preparation of the third and fourth. He had already assembled a hundred or more volumes of sources for further study when his efforts were ended by his death on February 25, 1933. Much of the material with which these next volumes were to have dealt has already appeared in other forms: in his *Protestant Thought Before Kant, The Rise of Modern Religious Ideas,* and in various periodicals. All this subject matter he proposed to rewrite on the basis of extended investigations. In presenting it he expected to use the same method of exposition in furtherance of the same objective that had controlled the first two volumes. His aim was to write not a history of the Christian church nor a history of the Christian religion nor a biographical history. He would have dealt with individuals not as men but as thinkers, their careers interesting him not at all, however great they might be, except insofar as they determined the person's thinking. What he proposed to write was a history of Christian Thought.

Throughout his academic life and more particularly after he became president of Union Theological Seminary my father was invited to deliver addresses, series of lectures, sermons and chapel talks. It is from this voluminous body of material which exists in manuscript and typescript, written out in full or preserved in outline only, that the present volume has been composed.

The principle of editorial selection has been two-fold. On the one hand I have sought to make available cer-

tain illuminating historical studies. At least one of
them, Christianity Old and New, had been partially
prepared by my father for publication. My second
purpose has been to set forth in general outline his own
interpretation of Christianity. As an historian he insisted on keeping his own views out of sight, often to
the exasperation of his students, who wanted to know
what he himself thought. Yet he had his own views
and expressed them freely and clearly when occasion
called for them, as the present volume indicates.

My editorial opportunity has been not only one of
selection but of arrangement also. I have endeavoured
to present both the major emphases and the unified
character of my father's theology. With this end in
view I have arranged the chosen material under section
headings devised to indicate both the root and the fruit
of his religion. I have resisted the temptation to include brilliant short excerpts from addresses which for
reasons of space could not be included as a whole. I
have refrained from using material excellent in itself
but which had no definite connection with the general
scope of this book. Each address, in the form of a
chapter, is given in its complete form, with an occasional
change here and there on minor points that in no wise
alters the meaning. The volume includes none of the
forty-three articles which my father published in addition to his ten books.

In a series of notes on page 313, I have mentioned
the dates and the occasions of the several addresses
insofar as they are ascertainable. To Mr. William L.

Savage of Charles Scribner's Sons, I wish to express my hearty appreciation for his good counsel in the preparation of this book.

ARTHUR CUSHMAN MCGIFFERT, JR.

CHICAGO THEOLOGICAL SEMINARY.

CONTENTS

Part I. History

Part II. A Contemporary Faith

CONTENTS

Part I

HISTORY

Chapter I

WHAT IS THE CHRISTIAN RELIGION?

AN HISTORICAL APPROACH TO THE QUESTION

Almost from the beginning, one of the extraordinary things about Christianity has been its great variety. To the apostle Paul, to Ignatius of Antioch, and to thousands of believers since, a religion of redemption, releasing men from the trammels of the world and sin and death, and giving them the power of an endless life. To Justin Martyr, to Pelagius, to Socinus, a revelation of God's will which we have abundant ability to obey if we but choose, and obeying which we reap the fitting reward. To Clement of Alexandria, to Scotus Eriugena, to G. Wilhelm Friedrich Hegel, to speculative thinkers of every age, a philosophy of the universe, explaining the whence and the whither, the beginning and the end of all things. To the schoolmen, both Catholic and Protestant, the acceptance of a series of propositions, supposed to contain final and absolute truth touching God and man and the universe. To St. Bernard and Fénelon and William Law, to the mystics of all generations, the transcendence of human limitations in oneness with the divine. To St. Francis of

Assisi and Thomas à Kempis, and many a lovely spirit of our own and other days, the imitation of Christ in his life of poverty, humility, and love. To Cyprian and Augustine and countless Catholics, the one holy, apostolic church, an ark of salvation, alone providing escape from eternal punishment. To Hildebrand and Innocent, as to modern ultramontanists in general, the papal hierarchy, ruler of the nations of the earth. To Benedict of Nursia, to Boniface the Saxon apostle, to not a few missionaries of these latter days, a great civilizing agency, raising whole peoples from ignorance and savagery to culture and humaneness. To the rationalist of the eighteenth century, the religion of nature always one and unchanging, the worship of God and the pursuit of virtue. To a growing multitude of Christians of our own day, humanitarianism, and the service of one's fellows in the spirit of Jesus Christ.

These were not simply different phases of the same faith, these were often altogether different faiths. They were not the mere development of an original principle, the life and work and teaching of Jesus of Nazareth, they were many of them fresh creations.

The explanation of this variety of interpretations of Christianity is to be found in the fact that Christianity is a world religion, spreading among different peoples and entering into the heritage of all sorts of racial traditions and habits of life and thought; and also in the fact that it has always been the vital faith of individuals and not merely a public or national cult. Out of varied human experiences, determined by education, by example, by individual temperament and character, new ways of looking at things arose, often so unlike Christ's that he could not have recognized them as interpretations of his own faith or his own ideals. The apostle Paul is an outstanding example. Though he perhaps understood Jesus better than any of his contemporaries, and certainly did more for the spread of his influence, he drew his gospel largely from an experience and philosophy wholly unlike Christ's. The feverish effort to keep the law, the terrible struggle with sin, the despair born of failure, the conclusion, confirmed by the dualistic metaphysics of the day that human nature is necessarily evil, the discovery of a redemptive significance in the birth and death and resurrection of Christ—this was no mere unfolding of the teaching of Jesus, no mere interpretation of his gospel. Paul, himself, was in it, and Paul was an original centre of creative force, as Jesus had been before him.

In any estimate of the Christian religion these varied and often entirely unrelated forms must be taken account of. To bring to our investigation a preconceived notion of Christianity and exclude from consideration those who do not conform to type would be to employ the dogmatic rather than the historical approach. We have no right to confine our study to the official pronouncements of any church or of all the churches. Our picture, if it be adequate and just, must include the Christianity not only of all sects but of all individuals, for Christianity is a personal and not merely an institutional religion. Are there then any common qualities beyond the mere name which bind them together and make them in any real sense one?

We call Christianity a religion and it would seem that we might fairly assume that, whatever their differences in other matters, all Christians at any rate worship the same God. Have we not then in the Christian God a means of determining the nature of Christianity and of distinguishing it from the other great religions of the world?

A notable historical fact is the extraordinary variety in the objects of Christian worship. Christian theism has taken all sorts of forms. I will not dwell upon the doubt that inevitably besets the historian whether all Christians have actually been theists, whether there have not been some forms of Christianity, as truly as of Buddhism, without any personal god. But I do wish to remind you that Christian theologians as well as laymen have often been genuine and thoroughgoing dualists, and that the religious experience of multitudes of devout and faithful disciples has found congenial expression in a polytheism as real as that of ancient Greece or Rome.

Still further, as is well known to all of us, even where Christianity has been completely monotheistic, or partially so, the one God or the supreme God worshipped by Christians has borne the most diverse characters. The great All, impersonal and without passions, or the ruler of the world, as individual as any man; the source of all good, or almighty and arbitrary will; an absentee God, or an indwelling spirit; a king to whom we must submit, or a father who loves us and whom we love; a God of wrath, or a God of mercy; a God both wrathful and merciful; an avenging God and a gracious Christ; the creator of the universe, or a being who works for the promotion of good in a world he has not made, or for the salvation of men from such a world.

There is no common quality in these various gods of Christian history beyond the mere name God, and few of them are peculiarly Christian. It may be said that the God of Christianity is the God of Jesus, and is to be distinguished from the gods of the Greeks and Confucianists and Hindus by that fact. But who was the God of Jesus? All the different Gods of Christian history have been supposed by their worshippers to be the God of Jesus. And while we may use his teaching to aid us in framing our conception of God, or in determining which of the many gods worshipped by Christians is the true God, to say that the God of Christian history is the God of Jesus does not help us in our present task. The unity thereby attained is merely verbal.

If we shall say that though the teaching of Jesus has been widely misinterpreted, still we have at least in theory a common factor which binds all Christians together, attention may be called to the fact that even in theory the teaching of Jesus has no greater authority for multitudes of Catholics than the teaching of Pius XI, and for multitudes of Protestants than the teaching of the Bible, Old Testament and New.

We can thus hardly do otherwise than conclude that there is no such oneness in the theisms of Christian history as to help us to a definition of the Christian religion.

If we cannot find what we seek in the theistic sphere, may we find it in the ethical?

Christianity is commonly called one of the great ethical religions of the world, like Confucianism, Buddhism, Judaism, and Mohammedanism. But is there anything different in its ethics, anything that marks it off from the others? As a matter of fact when we study Christian history we find almost as much disagreement here as in the theistic field. Speaking generally we may say that morality, or virtue, has always had some place in the Christian religion, but the place assigned to it has varied greatly. Now it has been made a mere means to something else, again it has been made itself the end. Here it has been regarded as a condition of salvation, there as the fruit of it. By some it has been thought of as the expression of the divine life in man, by others as a purely human thing. At times religion and ethics have been sharply sundered, at times they have been completely identified.

So too, ethical motives have been widely different: to please Christ, to glorify God, to live worthily of one's calling, to promote the good repute of Christianity, to influence others, to benefit society, to gain eternal reward and escape eternal punishment, to cultivate one's higher nature; and often true Christian virtue has been represented as wholly instinctive, the spontaneous and unmotived expression of Christian character.

And not simply the motives but the ideals of historic Christianity have frequently been totally opposed to each other: holiness or love; personal purity or service of one's fellows; asceticism or self-expression; otherworldliness or adaptation to this world; revolt against one's environment or harmony with it; separation from society or devotion to society's good; religious practices, or humanitarianism pure and simple; bondage or freedom, and in some forms of Christianity even antinomianism and libertinism. It is impossible to frame an ideal which shall include all these conflicting ideals, or to discover a common principle which underlies them and binds them all together.

Nor can we say that they are the fruit of Christianity and peculiar to it. Many of them are common human ideals, found in all religions and wholly apart from religion. Some of them are due to individual or racial temperament, to physical geography or climate, to the vicissitudes of war, to the development or decadence of industry and commerce. Their prevalence within the Christian church can often be traced directly to pre-Christian or non-Christian influences; in some cases, as for instance modern humanitarianism, one of the impulses which originally led to its emphasis was hostility to Christianity.

If we construct what we regard as the true Christian ideal, or the ideal of Jesus himself, we shall find, whatever it may be, that it has not been shared by all Christians or groups of Christians, that, on the contrary, it has been repudiated either explicitly or implicitly by many of them. It would seem then that though we may agree that historic Christianity is an ethical religion in the sense that moral conduct has always had, at least theoretically, some place in it, this fact gives us little help in reaching a definition of the Christian religion which shall distinguish it in nature or character from the other great religions of the world.

In the third place it may be asked, if Christianity has not always been a religion of salvation, and if in this fact we may not find a common element which will help us toward the definition we are seeking? The word salvation has been common in the Christian vocabulary of all the centuries and without question we can usually get at the very heart of a theologian's Christianity by asking what salvation meant to him. But even so there are here too diversities of interest and of interpretation which make difficulties for us.

How shall we bring under a common formula, or discover a common principle controlling such inconsistent notions of salvation as those of Irenæus, of Theophilus of Antioch, of Gregory the Great, of Amalric of Bena, of Martin Luther, of Giordano Bruno, of Matthew Tindal, of Jonathan Edwards, of Immanuel Kant, and of Friedrich Schleiermacher? And what justification is there for using the same word salvation to connote the controlling interest at once of the old-fashioned evangelical and of the modern humanitarian, or Christian socialist, with his complete indifference or agnosticism regarding a future life and with his interpretation of the kingdom of God as improved social, economic, and industrial conditions here and now? The most we can say is that both believe, as all Christians believe, that Christianity confers benefits of one kind or another upon men; but this every religion does, in the opinion of its adherents, and hence the belief fails to assist us in defining the nature of the Christian religion.

Once more, it may be asked, if we have not in the very name Christian, connecting our religion as it does with an historic figure, Jesus Christ, a common element which distinguishes Christianity from all the other religions of the world?

Unfortunately here too the common element is little more than verbal. To the early Jewish disciples Jesus was the promised Messiah, but to the Christians of subsequent centuries the Messianic category meant little or nothing even when the historic connection of the new with the old religion was recognized, as it was not, for instance, by the Gnostics.

Many have asserted that Jesus was a mere man, others that he was Very God of Very God. Some have interpreted his teachings and his purposes in one way, others in exactly opposite ways, so that in one age he has been made to stand for things which in the next were unqualifiedly condemned. Some have thought it impossible to discover what his teachings and purposes were; others that he never taught and worked at all. Most Christians have regarded him as the founder of Christianity, but some have ascribed that honor to others, particularly to Paul. He has been recognized as authoritative, but some have found his authority expressed in the Gospels, some in the Bible as whole, some in the church, while others have appealed to the inner light, either as supplementing or as supplanting his commands. And even where his authority has been made most of it has really meant as a rule only the binding character of whatever a particular age or a particular body of Christians has counted good and true.

We may say that Christians are those who worship Christ, or if they do not worship him, as many have not done, those who recognize him as master, or leader, or ideal, or inspiration or something of the kind, and that Christians do this is a fact of great practical importance, giving us a high name to win our victories with. But so long as Christ and his ideals and purposes are so differently interpreted, so long as estimates of him range all the way from a mere man to a God who has had no earthly life at all, we can hardly find in his figure a principle of definition such as we are seeking, a means of discovering the real nature of the Christian religion as an historical phenomenon.

I must not carry this discussion further. My conclusions, it is evident, are almost wholly negative. Christian history shows us, in my opinion, that Christianity has not

been one thing but many and often contradictory things
—and this simply means that there is no such thing as
Christianity in general—though there are many particular Christianities. The word Christianity taken by itself is a mere abstraction. There is John's Christianity,
and Wesley's Christianity, and Channing's Christianity,
but there is no universal Christianity, which we may
define, whose nature we may study, or whose essence
we may set forth. History abundantly teaches us that
the best we can do—and it is a thing well worth doing,
both on scientific and practical grounds—is to formu-
late our own Christianity, yours and mine and that of
the group to which we belong.

Section B

CHRISTIANITY OLD AND NEW

CHRISTIANITY OLD AND NEW

INTRODUCTION

In the following series of chapters on Christianity, Old and New, I have it in mind to attempt to answer two questions: Just how did traditional Christianity—Catholic and Protestant—come to be? and second, How has it been modified by modern thought? The series is intended to be exclusively historical, as my business is that of an historian, and I shall avoid expressing an opinion on the truth or falsity of the various ideas which will pass in review before us.

It would be futile, of course, to attempt a general history of Christian thought in four chapters. All I can expect to do is to indicate with such accuracy and clearness as I may the controlling ideas of the periods and churches with which I deal, the ideas which may be regarded as constituting the essence of their Christian faith. I hope to set these out briefly and concisely in their historic sequence and to show how the later grew out of or related themselves to the earlier interpretations.

CHAPTER II

PRIMITIVE CHRISTIANITY

The conversion of Saul of Tarsus meant the birth of a new religion which became Judaism's bitterest foe and was chiefly responsible for the ultimate disappearance of what we know as Jewish Christianity.

I cannot stop to trace the genesis and development of Paul's Christian faith out of which the new religion sprang. I may simply say that he found in Jesus Christ a saviour from sin and death and that he became the propagandist not of Jewish Messianism but of a new religion of personal salvation wholly divorced from Judaism and open on equal terms to all the peoples of the earth.

The heart of this new religion of Paul's was the belief that Jesus Christ is a divine being who by his death and resurrection saves those that are united to him by faith. The kinship of this new religion was with the mystery-cults which were playing so large a part in the religious life of the Roman world. With all their variety these mystery-cults agreed in promising to their adherents salvation from death and the enjoyment of a blessed immortality through union with the divine lord of the cult, dead and risen again.

Whether Paul got his interpretation of Christ and

his work from these mystery-cults or not, at any rate it was a genuine mystery-religion he was preaching, with its promise of salvation through a dying and risen Lord and with its guarantee of a blessed immortality for those initiated into the sacred company by baptism and mystically united to the divine Christ by participation in the eucharist.

It was as a mystery-religion—as mystery-religions were understood in those days—that Christianity conquered the Roman Empire. As a Jewish Messianic sect it could not possibly have had the vogue and won the victory it did. But Christianity was no ordinary mystery-religion; it was distinguished from all the other contemporary cults by its large admixture of Judaism; for not simply were Jesus and his personal disciples Jews but Paul too was a Hebrew of the Hebrews and he retained to the day of his death a considerable part of the faith of his fathers. Indeed, though we must recognize that he was the founder of a new mystery-cult, he believed himself to be a loyal Jew and the religion which he championed the true Judaism for which the traditional Jewish system had been in the providence of God a preparation. Thus he continued to worship the God of the Jews, the righteous creator, ruler and judge of the world, and though he added the Lord Jesus Christ as a second divine being he never faltered in his allegiance to the God of his fathers; Jesus Christ was no independent deity but the son of the God whom Paul had always worshipped.

Paul retained also his belief in the Jewish scriptures

as the word of God and in the covenant of God with his chosen people; and he shared the ethical ideals of the Jews, modifying them to some extent under the influence of the current asceticism of the day, which was the fruit of an estimate of human nature substantially identical with his own.

It is true that the converts whom Paul won in various provinces of the Roman Empire were by no means all of them in full sympathy with him. Attracted by his gospel of salvation many of them were content to accept Jesus Christ as their saviour, whether from sin or the world or death, without accepting the God of the Jews or the rest of the Jewish heritage which meant so much to Paul. Some of them had difficulties with the Jewish scriptures and with the character of the Jewish God portrayed therein; some of them were unable to retain so much of the old system while rejecting circumcision and the Jewish ceremonial law as their fellow Christians were doing; some of them shared the widespread prejudice against Judaism and thought it scandalous that the new religion should have anything in common with it; some of them were thoroughgoing dualists and were unable to identify the God whom they worshipped with the creator of the world—this evil world, salvation from which is the greatest need of man. To such Christians as these Christianity was a new thing in the world, wholly independent of Judaism and with no relation to the older faith.

Gradually however, in spite of the difficulties referred to, Paul's view prevailed and it came to be recognized that the Christian God is the God of the Jews and the sacred scriptures of the Jews the Christian Bible. Ultimately this became the alone orthodox belief and those who denied it were condemned as heretics and excluded from the Christian brotherhood.

Whatever the influences that led to this result it was historically speaking a happy result for the new religion. Deprived of its Jewish heritage Christianity would have been no more than one of the many mystery-cults of the age and must inevitably have perished with them. It might be thought that the personality of Jesus was alone enough to distinguish this cult from the others and to make it infinitely superior to them. Speaking abstractly this of course was true. But unfortunately the personality of Jesus meant little to the early Gentile Christians. The chief thing about him was that he had died and risen again, as the lords of the other cults had done, and his character and personality, when thought about at all, were altogether secondary. This was true in a measure even of Paul, Jew as he was; it was truer still of many others. There were large numbers indeed who even denied that Christ was a man at all; he was a divine being who had appeared temporarily on earth and had then ascended again to the place whence he came, his supposed sufferings and death, like his birth and human life, being only an illusion. Had it not been for the Jewish disciples whose controlling interest was wholly different from that of the mysteries, we should hardly be in possession of any records of Jesus' life and teaching, and should know him. if we knew him at all, only as a divine spirit, the lord of a cult.

The real superiority of Christianity to other cults, which accounted for its ultimate victory, was due primarily to its Jewish heritage. Its God was the creator, ruler, and judge of the world, a righteous God demanding righteousness in his worshippers. Thus Christianity was given a cosmological and an ethical character unmatched in any other cult. As the heir of Judaism it also appropriated to itself the immense prerogatives to which the Jews had laid claim, interpreting all history as a preparation for the appearance of the new Israel, the true people of God. Offensive as such enormous pretensions were to many an outsider (as, for example, to Celsus and to Cæcilius, one of the interlocutors in the *Octavius* of Minucius Felix), they proved immensely attractive to multitudes and gave the new religion an unexampled strength.

In the Jewish scriptures the Christians had a religious classic unapproached in Greek literature for variety and convincingness of appeal and for the beauty and moving quality of its devotional passages. To be sure it too was offensive to many of the most religious spirits of the age because of its mythology, the primitive nature of much of its theism, its often questionable ethics, its ritual requirements, its racial self-consciousness, and its narrow and bitter nationalism. But at worst there was much in it to set against all this, and read allegorically, as was the custom of the age with religious classics, its defects were minimized; while its prophecies, when it was reinterpreted in Christian terms, as it early was, supplied the church with an armory of apologetic weapons surpassing anything to be found elsewhere.

As part of Christianity's heritage from Judaism must be reckoned also its greatest propagandist, the apostle Paul. Christianity as an independent religion owed its origin to him, and antipathetic as he was to multitudes both Jews and Greeks, he had that rare combination of burning conviction, practical efficiency, and speculative genius that made him one of the great religious builders of history. Nowhere else among the mystery-cults of antiquity was there a figure of his creative and compelling power.

To all this is to be added the figure of Jesus himself —of the man Jesus as conceived not by his Gentile but by his Jewish disciples and preserved for the admiration and devotion of his followers in every age. Denying its Jewish ancestry Christianity would have had to do without the human Jesus and would have had to content itself with the divine Lord of the cult, a sorry substitute for the man of the Gospels. As it was, Jesus' character and example were embalmed in the Gospels and handed down to later generations, and, though all too commonly obscured by Christology and sacramentarianism, became the most notable of all the distinguishing features of the new faith.

In view of what has been said it is not surprising that Christianity, though but one of the many mystery-religions abroad in the Roman Empire, should have survived them all and won its way to victory. With a dying and risen Lord it had everything that any of them could offer, and because its Lord was Jesus Christ and its greatest missionary the apostle Paul, and because it retained permanently the stamp of its Jewish origin, it was infinitely superior to the best of them.

As I have said, it was not as a Messianic movement but as a religion of personal salvation that Christianity won its victory in the Roman world. But there was a considerable variety of opinion as to what this salvation was and how much it included.

It was agreed by all that the salvation promised by Christianity meant escape from death and the enjoyment of a blessed immortality. The words of Second Clement are representative: "Let not the godly be grieved if he be miserable in the times that now are; a blessed time awaiteth him. He shall live again with the fathers and shall have rejoicing throughout a sorrowless eternity."[1]

Whether this eternal life, as it was called, began here and included the present existence of the believer, as Paul maintained, or whether it commenced only after death, as was generally thought, in either case it was the very heart of the Christian proclamation. Whatever else it might be Christianity was a religion promising eternal life—a future life of blessedness to be spent in communion with God, Christ, and the saints, a life crowned with piety and holiness and knowledge of the truth and freed from suffering and sorrow of every

[1] 2 Clem., chap. 19.

kind. The future life, it was believed, surpasses the present not only in excellence but also in duration. Permanence, imperishability, unchangeableness are the qualities most often spoken of in contrast with the brevity, impermanence, and changeableness of the present life. Sometimes this eternal life was described in sensuous terms, as in certain apocalypses, but it is a remarkable fact that almost invariably in our early literature it is given a genuinely spiritual connotation.

There were many, commonly known as Chiliasts, who thought of salvation as assuring to Christian believers not only eternal life in heaven but also, as a preliminary thereto, the enjoyment of the blessings of an earthly kingdom to be set up at the return of Christ and to continue for a thousand years until the final judgment and the end of the world. Thus Justin Martyr says: "I and others who are right-minded are assured that there will be a resurrection of the flesh and a thousand years in Jerusalem which will then be built and adorned and enlarged as the prophets Ezekiel and Isaiah and others declare."[2] Similarly Papias of Hierapolis, a contemporary of Justin's, says: "There will be a period of some thousand years after the resurrection of the dead and the Kingdom of Christ will be set up in material form on this very earth."[3]

This Jewish belief appears in the apocalypses of John and Peter and was shared by Irenæus and many other early Christians, but it was gradually outgrown

---

[2] *Dialogue with Trypho,* chap. 80.
[3] Eusebius, *Church History,* III, 39:12; *cf.* Irenæus, *Against Heresies,* V, 33:4.

as the expected return of Christ was delayed, and the espousal of it by the sect of the Montanists in the latter part of the second century promoted its unpopularity. Finally it came to be generally regarded as a heresy, a survival of Jewish error and the peculiar foible of the vulgar and ignorant mind. Over and over again it has reappeared in history but has never attained to the dignity of orthodox doctrine, either Catholic or Protestant.

Again it was agreed by all—whether they were Chiliasts or not—that Christianity promises salvation from the present evil world. "The friendship of the world is enmity with God" according to the Epistle of James, and the author of I John declares "If any man love the world the love of the Father is not in him." The author of Second Clement, after quoting the words of Jesus "No servant can serve two masters" and "What doth it profit a man if he gain the whole world and lose his own soul?" continues, "Now this age and the future are two enemies. The one speaketh of adultery and defilement and avarice and deceit, but the other biddeth farewell to these. We cannot therefore be friends of the two, but must bid farewell to one and hold companionship with the other. Let us consider that it is better to hate the things which are here, because they are mean and for a short time and perishable, and to love the things which are there, for they are good and imperishable."[4]

Sometimes Satan was represented as the ruler of the

---

[4] 2 Clem. 6.

present world as God is the ruler of the world to come. Paul even called him "the god of this world";[5] and the author of the so-called Epistle of Barnabas declared that "the one (*i.e.*, God) is Lord from all eternity and unto all eternity, whereas the other (*i.e.*, Satan) is Lord of the season of iniquity that now is."[6] In accordance with this idea human life appears in some of the documents as the scene of a conflict between the powers of light and the powers of darkness, each of which is striving for the mastery over man. According to Paul "Our wrestling is not against flesh and blood, but against the principalities, against the powers, against the world rulers of this darkness, against the spiritual hosts of wickedness in the heavenly places."[7] And Hermas has considerable to say about the good and evil angels or good and evil spirits who are with men, leading them into righteousness or wickedness. That Jesus Christ was able to overcome Satan and the many evil demons that infest the world was one of the established convictions of the early Christians and one of the reasons for calling him Lord.

The early Christian view of the present world was commonly pessimistic in the extreme; evil and soon to pass away, the one thing to be desired was to escape from it and attain the glory of the world that was to be. Not harmony with one's environment but revolt against it was the ideal at any rate of most Christians; not a world-affirming but a world-renouncing ethic they believed in.

The ideal of social service was wholly lacking. Not

---

[5] 2 Cor. 4:4.   [6] Barnabas, chap. 18.   [7] Eph. 6:12.

the amelioration of society, not the service of the world, but one's own salvation was the supreme end of life, and if charity and kindliness and generosity were recognized as Christian virtues they were commonly practised more for one's own sake than for the sake of others.

Under the influence of the Hellenistic dualism of the age Paul interpreted salvation as escape from the flesh which is radically evil and cannot be redeemed; the life of the saved man is spiritual only, not fleshly. In this he was followed by the Gnostics and Marcionites, as also by the great Origen of Alexandria, but to the mass of Christians such salvation seemed too tenuous to be real and they insisted upon the literal resurrection of the flesh, following in this the Jewish tradition rather than the Greek. The author of Second Clement puts the matter in the following explicit terms: "Let none of you say that this flesh is not judged and does not rise again. Understand: In what were you saved, in what did you regain your sight if not in this flesh? We must therefore guard the flesh as a temple of God; for as you were called in the flesh, in the flesh also shall you come. If Christ the Lord who saved us, though at first spirit, became flesh and so called us, thus also we shall receive the reward in this flesh."[8]

This Jewish belief finds expression in the Apostles' Creed, which says in the original not "resurrection of the body," as in our English translation, but "resurrection of the flesh." The following interesting passage from Irenæus, the great anti-Gnostic writer of the sec-

[8] 2 Clem. 9.

ond century, shows how this view was reconciled with the very different view of Paul. "If therefore it is flesh and blood that give us life it has not been said of flesh and blood in a literal sense that they cannot inherit the kingdom of heaven [as Paul says in I Cor. 15:50] but the words refer to the above-mentioned carnal deeds which turn man to sin and deprive him of life."[9]

The truth is, Paul's view easily lent itself to misunderstanding for it retained the framework of the doctrine of the resurrection while the substance of it was Hellenistic not Jewish. According to Paul this body of ours is not raised but a new spiritual body is given us suited to our new spiritual existence, and this is in essence of course not resurrection at all but immortality.

Again it was generally believed that the salvation offered by Christianity meant escape from everlasting punishment which in the future world was to be inflicted upon unbelievers who were to suffer in the very bodies in which they had sinned. As Justin Martyr puts it: "Plato used to say that Rhadamanthus and Minos would punish the wicked who came before them. We say that the same thing will be done, but at the hands of Christ and upon the wicked existing in the same bodies which they now have, which will then be raised with their spirits for everlasting punishment and not only, as Plato said, for a punishment of a thousand years."[10]

[9] *Against Heresies*, V, 14:4.   [10] Justin Martyr, *Apol.* I. 8.

Among the Zoroastrians, from whom the Jews derived the belief in the resurrection and in the future punishment of the wicked, the punishment was thought of as temporary only and remedial, but among the Jews it was usually considered as everlasting, as it was also among the Christians. Paul too believed in the judgment and punishment of the wicked but he based his assurance of eternal life solely upon the believer's union with Christ and there was therefore no foundation in his theory for the resurrection of the wicked or for their continued existence after death. How he would have resolved the inconsistency we do not know.

The belief in the judgment and future punishment which was shared by many pagans as well as Jews and Christians was repudiated by the Paulinist Marcion and his followers; they thought of God as a saviour only, not a judge. But the church at large regarded divine judgment as an essential part of the Christian faith, and the desire to escape the everlasting punishment to be inflicted upon the wicked and unbelieving became one of the most cogent motives for Christian discipleship.

I have been speaking of the variety of opinion touching the nature and content of salvation. Early Christians differed also as to the conditions of salvation. Some followed Paul in emphasizing mystical union with the divine Christ; others emphasized repentance and obedience. The two were given equal weight by Irenæus,[11] bishop of Lyons in the latter part of the sec-

[11] For an elaboration of Irenæus' doctrine of salvation, see McGiffert, *A History of Christian Thought*, Vol. I, pp. 134-48.

ond century, and taken all in all the most important theologian of the early church. He combined the mystical and the ethical in such a way as to give them both a permanent place in Christian theology.

Chapter III

CATHOLICISM

Christianity's heritage from Judaism included the belief that the adherents of the new religion were the chosen people of God, heirs of the divine covenant made long before with the children of Israel. It was in this sense that the word Church or the phrase Church of God was used by Paul and became current in early Christian literature. The word became the standing designation of the new movement. It was used both of the movement as a whole—as the phrase People of God also was—and of individual congregations. The former was primary and fundamental, the local churches being thought of not as independent entities but as manifestations of the one Church of God which was older than they and from which they derived their character and significance. This appears for instance in Paul's Epistles to the Corinthians which are addressed to "the Church of God which is at Corinth."[1]

This Church of God was thought of just as their church was thought of by the Jews, not as a human but as a divine institution, created by God not man. It was he who had called Christians out of the world to be his peculiar people, and he had called them not for the sake of the world but for his own sake and theirs.

[1] *Cf.* also I Cor. 15:9.

The church indeed, according to some of the early
Christians, is older than the world and for its sake the
world was framed. As the author of Second Clement
puts it: "If we do the will of our Father we shall belong to the first church, the spiritual, which was created before the sun and moon."[2] With which may be
compared the following striking passage from the Shepherd of Hermas: "While I slept a revelation was made
to me, brethren, by a very beautiful youth who said to
me, 'Who do you think the old lady is from whom you
received the little book?' 'The Sybil,' I replied. 'You
are wrong,' he said, 'it is not she.' 'Who then is it?' I
asked. 'The Church,' he replied. 'Why then is she
old?' I asked. 'Because,' he said, 'she was created first
of all things; therefore she is old, and for her sake the
world was made.' "[3]

The tremendous power of such a conception as this
may be easily imagined. It is evident that where such
an idea prevailed the church was something more than
the mere sum of Christian believers; as it was older
than the several local churches scattered over the empire so it was older than all its members. They did
not make it; it made them. Entering it they became
children of God and a part of his chosen people.

In early days little seems to have been demanded of
those who wished to enter the Christian church except
the recognition of Christ as Lord; but as time passed
radical differences emerged which led to a serious crisis
and resulted ultimately in the formation of the Catho-

[2] 2 Clem. 14.   [3] Hermas, *Vision*, II. 4.

lic church and its separation from all other Christian bodies. These differences were due chiefly to the rejection by many Gentile Christians of the Jewish elements which principally distinguished Christianity from the other mystery-cults of the age and to which I referred in the previous chapter. In the controversy that resulted, commonly known as the Gnostic controversy, Irenæus took a prominent part and in the course of it formulated the conception of the Catholic church which has remained normative ever since. Supplemented and enlarged by Callixtus, bishop of Rome, and Cyprian, bishop of Carthage, this conception was already complete in all its essential features by the middle of the third century and from that time on the lines were sharply drawn between the Catholic church and all other groups of Christians, of which there were many scattered over the empire east and west. The Catholic church ultimately won the victory over these other groups because it preserved better than any of them at once the Jewish and the Hellenistic elements in the new religion.

This Catholic church has existed from that day to this. It has passed through many vicissitudes but it is still strong and vigorous. In the Middle Ages it split into two parts, the Greek and the Roman, each retaining the characteristics of the parent stem and each claiming to be alone the true Catholic church. The genius of Catholicism may be studied in either of these churches, but as the Roman Catholic is more familiar to us and as in it certain features of Catholicism have found larger and more consistent expression than in the Greek church, I may fairly confine myself to it in this chapter. I shall speak of it without more ado simply as the Catholic church, not only for convenience sake but also because much of what I have to say applies in almost equal measure to both Greek and Roman Catholicism.

Fundamental in both eastern and western Catholicism is the conviction inherited from primitive Christianity that the Catholic church is of divine not human origin. However much human genius and energy may have had to do with its formation it is believed to have come from God; and not simply that, it is believed also to be under constant divine control and guidance, the body of which Christ is the head, and in which the Holy Spirit dwells. It is supernatural not natural, and it demands reverence and obedience. This divine and supernatural church is a saving institution, founded for the purpose of rescuing from the world and sin and death perishing souls who are quite unable to rescue themselves. In the previous chapter I spoke of ideas of salvation and the means of salvation current in the early church, and I need not dwell further upon the matter here. I may simply say that the salvation offered by the Catholic church has always been an essentially individualistic and other-worldly thing; not social but personal, not the transformation of this world and its institutions into the kingdom of God, but the enjoyment of eternal blessedness in another world beyond the grave. Because of this the church was ill-fitted for the rôle of a state-church when that rôle was thrust upon it. In monasticism rather than in statesmanship the Christian spirit was believed to find its highest expression.

The theory of the church as a supernatural saving institution found expression in the doctrine of the sacraments. More and more as time passed the sacraments were put in the forefront and became the characteristic feature of Catholic Christianity. Without the divine grace imparted through them human effort is quite vain and salvation wholly unattainable. The natural man remains a child of perdition; only when supernaturally endowed and empowered can he so live as to win the reward of future blessedness.

In genuine sacramentarianism this transformation is supposed to take place below the level of consciousness. It is essentially a physical rather than an ethical process, but it has important ethical results in purified desires and renewed wills. Sacramentarianism is bound up with the belief that the physical and the mental are intimately connected and mutually dependent. This is a common belief today and it is widely recognized that the subconscious has large influence on the conscious. Sacramentarianism is therefore not without analogies in everyday human life. But in sacramentarianism the physical substratum is assumed to be of supernatural instead of natural origin and thus to be altogether beyond the reach of psychological analysis.

Whatever may be thought of the sacramental theory —which is of the very essence of Catholicism—at any rate it is evident that the belief in the efficacy of the sacraments is itself enough to work transformations in the character and disposition of the recipient, giving him the consciousness of enhanced moral ability and with it the power to live more nearly as he knows he ought to live. There is no possible doubt that the sacraments have actually been a means of grace to multitudes of Catholics in every age.

Though there may be many things we Protestants do not like about the Catholic church, we cannot fairly deny its claim to be a saving institution. That to many of us the salvation offered by it seems too self-centred and other-worldly and the means by which it is attained too materialistic may well be. I shall have occasion to refer to this aspect of the matter later. But this should not blind us to the fact that the Catholic church not only claims to be but has abundantly shown itself to be a saving institution. Through its ministrations multitudes have been made holier and happier; have been set free from the dominance of their passions; have had their ideals heightened and their moral power strengthened. In so far the Catholic church has made good and justly enjoys the reverence and affection of its members. To their satisfaction it has proved its saving power over and over again in every generation. It has offered not only escape for sin-sick souls but adventure and achievement for many eager and ambitious spirits—adventure and achievement in self-denial, in communion with God, in Christian discipleship, in the service of the church. Whatever the official theory of salvation it must be recognized that the actual experience of salvation within Catholicism has been infinitely rich and varied. "By their fruits ye shall know them," and the fruits of Catholicism are evident to all the world in countless beautiful and saintly lives.

The Catholic church both east and west claims not only to be a saving institution but also to have authority over the consciences and intellects of men, and the Roman Catholic church claims authority over all human institutions as well. The authority to declare the truth which Irenæus in the second century ascribed to the church Augustine in the fifth century broadened to include the authority to rule the world. According to him the *civitas terrena,* comprising the Roman Empire and all other states, is subject to the *civitas Dei,* the holy Catholic church. The theory which for some centuries remained only a theory found practical if incomplete and temporary realization in the papal church of the Middle Ages and is still a part of the papal ideal.

The authority of the Catholic church is due to the possession of divine truth committed to it by the Apostles and transmitted and conserved by the apostolic episcopate. The assumption is that truth is something absolute and eternal to which human life must conform. The problem for humanity is not to work out in daily experience the best ideals and ways of living but to discover the will of God who has created men and to fulfil whose purposes for them is their highest end. Right living therefore has as its necessary presupposition knowledge of the divine will and the determination to fulfil it at any cost to oneself or others. Christian ideals are supernatural and only a supernatural institution like the Catholic church is in a position to know and inculcate them. An essential part of right living is right thinking and whether in any particular case the connection between the one and the other is discernible or not it is as necessary to accept what the church teaches as it is to do what it directs. That one shall understand all the teachings of the church and intelligently make them one's own is not expected, except in the case of teachers and theologians, but that one shall trust the church and take for true everything it says is necessary to salvation. In other words the authority of the Catholic church is absolute and the true attitude toward it is complete submission. This has been insisted on ever since the time of Irenæus. The church is a supernatural and divine institution and it speaks with the authority of God.

To an outsider it seems that such a conception of the church must be an intolerable bondage and there have been times when it has seemed such to Catholics themselves, but as a rule it has worked the other way. To many a doubting and troubled mind the infallibility of the church has brought peace and contentment. Multitudes indeed have found in its authority the greatest comfort and have been attracted to the church by this more than by anything else. Cardinal Newman speaks for them when he describes the effects of his conversion to the Roman church: "From the time I became a Catholic . . . I have had no anxiety of heart whatever. I have been in perfect peace and contentment. I have never had one doubt . . . It was like coming into port after a rough sea."[4]

Augustine said: "I would not believe the gospel unless moved thereto by the authority of the Catholic Church."[5] That a man of his rich religious experience should make such a declaration is very significant. What must the church's authority have meant to less independent spirits than his?

It is difficult for many of us to appreciate the attractiveness of this kind of thing. Truth seems so essentially a matter for human investigation and discovery that the idea of looking to a supernatural source for it seems wholly alien. But to one who lives in the atmosphere of the supernatural, whose whole life is governed by the sense of it, supernatural authority is a matter of course and the want of it breeds constant restlessness and unhappiness. The need is not confined to Catholics; it is shared by many Protestants as well. And if it does not find satisfaction in an infallible church it will find it in an infallible Bible, or in direct divine revelation.

Again Catholicism is marked by the sense of antiquity. Regardless of the historic fact that the Catholic church—a particular institution distinguished from all other Christian groups—emerged only a century and a half or more after the time of Christ, it claims both in east and west to be coeval with Christianity and to have had the historic Jesus for its founder. Even

---

[4] *Apologia pro vita sua* (*Everyman* ed.), p. 215.
[5] *Against the Epistle of Manichæus*, 5.

apart from this its antiquity is imposing enough. No
other institution of the western world, ecclesiastical or
civil, can compare with it in this respect whether it be
actually nineteen centuries old or only seventeen. No
wonder the Catholic looks with pitying contempt upon
the countless ephemeral sects that mark our Protestant
Christendom.

Associated with its antiquity is its continuity: the persistence during all these centuries of the same spirit, the
same faith, the same ideals, and the same practices. To
be sure this continuity is partial only not complete. It
is the Catholic theory that all the essential features of
Catholicism can be traced back to the very beginning;
and the claim is much truer than Protestants as a rule
have been willing to admit. In their polemic zeal the
Reformers set the primitive over against the Catholic
church and insisted that the latter was a mediæval invention. We know now that they were largely wrong,
that the essential features of Catholicism even in its
Roman form long antedate the Middle Ages. At the
same time we know also that there has been a large development—particularly in the west, and that there is
much not only in practice but in faith as well that dates
from later centuries, for Catholicism has always been
a creative as well as a conserving force. Catholics justify these faiths and practices by claiming that they are
not actual novelties but were already present in the
mind of the apostles and emerged in the consciousness
of the church when the time was ripe for them.[6] This,

---

[6] *Cf.* Cardinal Newman's principle of development.

of course, is only an apologetic subterfuge, but it illustrates the sense of antiquity and continuity which has always marked Catholicism, the instinctive need of finding ancient and divine warrant for the whole range of Catholic life and thought. And in the present instance the apologetic subterfuge has more justification than usual for the new has not been artificially added to the old but has grown out of it by a natural process, so that genuine continuity has been preserved and old and new form parts of one organic whole. This must be kept in mind in every attempt to interpret the genius of Catholicism.

Again Catholicism is marked by universality and the spirit of inclusiveness. As was seen in the first chapter there went into the making of historic Catholicism both Judaism and Hellenism. Gnosticism was condemned not in the interest of an exclusive but of an inclusive Christianity. The syncretistic character of Gnosticism is often spoken of but the trouble with it was that it was not syncretistic enough, for while it was a complex of Hellenism and Orientalism it rejected Judaism altogether. Catholicism also incorporated the Orientalized Hellenism of the day on a large scale but it accepted Judaism as well and was thus more of a syncretism than Gnosticism itself. Because Gnosticism was too narrow it was condemned in the interest of a more inclusive faith. And this kind of thing has happened over and over again. In the fourth century Catholicism became the official religion of the Roman Empire and took over not only the old temples but also many of the old forms of religion and rites of worship. Indeed the history of Christianity for five hundred years was marked by the growing inclusion of religious practices and philosophical ideas from all sorts of sources.

Catholicism became a world-religion, the only religion generally known to the peoples of Europe during the Middle Ages, and as such it met the most diverse religious needs, the religious needs of every kind and class of men from the best to the worst, from the highest to the lowest, from the educated to the illiterate. If the traditional interpretation of Christianity failed to meet the needs of a new generation or of a people with a different background novel interpretations appeared and fresh forms and ceremonies emerged to fit the changed situation. Catholicism indeed for all its conservatism was continually developing and changing, at least in the west where new peoples were coming under its control. It did not slough off the old but it took on the new and became ever richer and more complex. No type of religious experience and few religious ideals have failed to find a home in Catholicism: legalism and mysticism, materialism and spiritualism, humility and pride, dependence and independence, self-indulgence and self-denial, egoism and altruism, activity and contemplation, sacramentarianism and rationalism, monotheism and polytheism, creationism and evolutionism. Inclusiveness has been a marked characteristic of Catholicism in every age. Not necessarily unlimited inclusiveness but a large measure of inclusiveness has made the church a home for all classes and peoples and for the widest variety of character and temperament, and this has been one of its greatest charms, particularly to those of broad vision and wide human interests.

Closely related to its inclusiveness is its unity. In spite of its immense variety and the widely different elements that are found within its capacious bosom it remains one institution, at least in its Roman form; not simply one in spirit and purpose but one in organization, with a single head ruling the whole, so that the Pauline figure of the body of Christ has found in it its realization to a degree approached nowhere else. The contrast between this unity and the disunity of Protestantism has been one of the great sources of Rome's strength and one of the most compelling factors in its appeal. The variety of religious temperament and of theological belief is probably as great in Roman Catholicism as in Protestantism, at any rate in the Protestantism of the historic denominations, and yet the Roman church has known how to preserve its external unity as the Protestant churches have not. The monastic orders have been a great help in this connection, providing places of refuge for many of the most creative and radical spirits who otherwise might have been driven to found new and independent sects. But more than all else is the overmastering devotion to the principle of unity itself which Cyprian put at the very heart of his doctrine of the church and which has never lost its central place for Catholic believers. Driven out of the Catholic church against their will it was impossible for

the Protestant Reformers to make as much of ecclesiastical unity as the Romanists were doing. As a matter
of fact unity was deliberately sacrificed by them, or the
sacrifice of it was deliberately accepted, in the interest
of what seemed more imperative, the purity of the
gospel.

In the unity of the Roman Catholic church many find
its most attractive feature, particularly in this age when
unity is the watchword of the hour. The impressiveness
of such an institution in contrast with our divided Protestantism gives it a power out of all proportion to its
numerical strength and its intellectual endowments, as
has been witnessed for instance since the war.

Thus far I have been speaking of what may be called
the positive features of Catholicism: its saving power,
its authority, its antiquity, its continuity, its creativeness,
its inclusiveness, and its unity; but it has also a negative aspect which is no less essential, for the Catholic
church, at least in its Roman form, claims to be the
only true church and denies that salvation is to be found
in any other. It might possess all the characteristics I
have described and yet count itself only one church or
one way of salvation among many. But this it has never
done. From the beginning the Catholic church has
claimed to be not merely a true church but the only
true church, not merely one way of salvation but the
only way. Indeed as already seen it was in distinguishing itself from all other forms of Christianity that
Catholicism had its birth.

The denial of salvation to any one outside the Catholic church was not an innovation, at least not in principle. The difference between Catholic and primitive Christianity was not that Catholicism was exclusive while primitive Christianity was not. "Outside the Church there is no salvation" was as generally believed among primitive Christians as among Catholics. Peter is reported to have said that salvation was impossible apart from Christ (Acts 4:12) and whether he actually said so or not his words represent the general opinion of the church at an early day.[7] To say there is salvation only in Christ is, of course, not explicitly to say that salvation is impossible outside the church, but this is what was meant. It was taken for granted that salvation was to be had only within the Christian circle. It is true that in early days as well as now there were those who held aloof and absented themselves from the services of the church to the scandal of their fellows; but they evidently belonged to the Christian circle, or in other words to the Christian church, and they can hardly have expected to be saved apart from it.

There was thus a note of exclusiveness in Christianity from the beginning. As Judaism was for the Jews, so Christianity was for the Christians, and as only those who belonged either by birth or adoption to the people of Israel were Jews, so only those who belonged to the Christian church were Christians.

How are we to explain this note of exclusiveness? Christianity, as I have said, was one of the mystery-

---

[7] *Cf.* the words ascribed to Jesus in John 14:6; as also in Matt. 11:27 and Luke 10:22.

religions of the ancient world; but in the other mystery-religions the note of exclusiveness was as a rule lacking.[8] It is to be explained I think as due primarily to the influence of Judaism. Where it was believed that the Christians were the true Israel of God who had supplanted the Jewish nation as God's chosen people the spirit of exclusiveness was natural. But this is not the whole of the matter. The historic connection of Christianity with Judaism and the recognition of the God of the Jews as the God of the Christians actually put the new religion into a class by itself and differentiated it from all the other mystery-cults which left the common polytheism of the day unmolested. The distinction in this respect between Christianity and the other cults strengthened the conviction that Christianity was not only superior but stood alone as the one and only way of salvation. This appears very clearly in the writings of the apologists of the second century as well as in Irenæus and Tertullian.

It is not strange that when certain second-century Christians who were generally known as Gnostics denied Christianity's connection with Judaism and repudiated its doctrine of one God the creator and ruler and judge of the world, thus reducing the new religion to the level of the other mystery-cults, they should seem to be destroying Christianity itself and should be denounced as anti-Christian. The inevitable result was Catholicism, the legitimate, indeed the only possible heir

8 The note of exclusiveness may also have been lacking for a time in some Gentile Christian groups: see McGiffert, *The God of the Early Christians*, pp. 46 f.

of primitive Christianity. The circumstances being what they were primitive exclusiveness could not do other than develop into Catholic exclusiveness.

The difference then between Catholic and primitive Christianity was not that Catholicism was exclusive while primitive Christianity was not; the note of exclusiveness was present from the beginning. The difference was in their definitions of the church, or perhaps it is better to say in the conditions demanded for membership in it. To the primitive Christian the church was the company of all those recognizing Christ as Lord and joining the group of his disciples; outside the church were only unconverted Jews and heathen. To the Catholic the church was a specific institution distinguished from other bodies that called themselves Christian, an institution organized in a particular way, the condition of membership in which was not simply the recognition of Christ as Lord but the acceptance of various propositions about God and Christ, the past and the future, and outside of it were not simply unconverted Jews and heathen but many who claimed to be Christians and as good Christians as any Catholic. From the Catholic point of view to be sure the Catholic church embraced all Christians as truly as the primitive church had done. But this was widely disputed by Christians themselves, many of whom denied altogether the identity of Catholicism and Christianity and this gave Catholicism an appearance of exclusiveness surpassing that of primitive Christianity and even that of Judaism. In principle however the situation was the same. To say that only Catholics can be saved is no more exclusive so far as spirit and attitude go than to say that only Christians can be saved.

This whole matter of exclusiveness, whether Christian or Catholic, is worthy of somewhat careful consideration, for its exact significance is often misunderstood. There are two kinds of exclusiveness, widely different from each other. The one is the exclusiveness of aristocracy which rests on the possession of prerogatives in the very nature of the case inaccessible to most people, as for instance an aristocracy of birth. This is essentially anti-social, the satisfaction involved depending on the difference between ourselves and others. If all were equally well born the satisfaction would disappear; or if anybody that wanted to could enter the charmed circle it would lose its significance altogether. In the religious realm this kind of exclusiveness is represented by Judaism; to the Jew belong by birth prerogatives denied to all the rest of the world. It is also represented by those Christian sects which hold the doctrine of unconditional election. Here the ground of special privilege is not birth but the divine will—an even more splendid distinction. The elect and the non-elect are eternally separated; there is no passing from the one class to the other.

This kind of exclusiveness is very easy to understand. It is so instinctive that it exists illogically even when there is little enough ground for it; even when the prerogatives on which one prides oneself are of questionable worth, or are easily accessible to others and are not universally shared only because they are not universally counted desirable. A man for instance is proud of being an Episcopalian and finds a certain satisfaction in being distinguished from others who belong to what seem to him less favored churches, though as a matter of fact anybody can be an Episcopalian that wants to. Similarly a man is proud of being a minister, or a lawyer, or what not; or he is even proud of living in Boston or New York; or of wearing certain kinds of clothes, or getting up at a certain hour in the morning, or eating a particular breakfast food. Any of these might be shared by everybody, but actually they are not and because of this they serve as marks of distinction from others and thus help the ego to maintain its reality and independence. The psychology of all this I say is very easy to understand.

But there is an exclusiveness of an altogether different type, often to be sure confounded with the kind I have been describing but easily distinguishable from it. It is this second kind that is exemplified in Christianity and particularly in Catholicism. Christianity is a missionary religion—as Catholicism is too—and this means that its adherents are interested to enlarge their borders and increase their numbers and thus in the end to break down rather than build up the distinction between themselves and others. The instinct here is social, not anti-social; the instinct to share the good we have rather than to monopolize it, to admit others to the privileges we enjoy rather than to hold ourselves aloof in our pride at possessing what they lack and cannot get. Psychologically the difference is radical and the practical results are wholly diverse. And yet the attitude is marked by thoroughgoing exclusiveness; within the Christian church alone or within the Catholic church alone is salvation possible. Such an attitude is no less exclusive because social in its interest rather than anti-social, or altruistic rather than selfish; but the exclusiveness is of another type and is secondary rather than primary. It is the fruit of one's estimate of one's religion rather than the root of it. If I may so express myself it is a democratic rather than an aristocratic exclusiveness, though the expression is not particularly illuminating. But what I mean is clear enough. In the one case we are exclusive because we want to emphasize the difference between ourselves and others; in the other case we are exclusive because we are impressed with the unique excellence of what we have to share with those who have it not. Such exclusiveness may be trying to those who think there are other ways of salvation than the Christian or the Catholic, but it is not unlovely as the other kind of exclusiveness is, and it is not to be condemned as of a piece with it.

The distinction I have drawn serves to explain the fact, puzzling enough to modern Protestants, that the Catholic church has contained so many beautiful Christian spirits filled with devotion to Christ and love for their fellows, who have yet been as intolerant as the extremest bigot in their insistence that salvation is possible only within the Catholic establishment. We can hardly associate the exclusiveness which I have called the exclusiveness of aristocracy with the humility of a St. Francis or a Thomas à Kempis but the other kind of exclusiveness they both had plenty of; they were good Catholics and believed that outside the Roman communion there was no salvation. The difficulty with their attitude—with Catholic exclusiveness as with Christian exclusiveness in general—is not that it is selfish or anti-social and hence unchristian, but that it is unenlightened. It interprets salvation and the way of salvation too narrowly and as a consequence lacks understanding for men of other faiths.

I have been speaking of Catholic exclusiveness at its best, but unfortunately it is seldom at its best for it is the kind of thing that lends itself all too easily to abuse. For one thing the conviction that our way of salvation is the only way is apt to foster unholy pride and contempt for all outside our own communion; and this is but another form of the exclusiveness of aristocracy, with its fundamentally unchristian spirit.

Then too we are apt to get interested in our way of salvation or in our church or sect, for its own sake and think more of it than of the human needs it is intended to serve. Not always of course but often other ways of salvation are condemned not because we fear for the safety of those who accept them, but because they detract from the credit of the remedy we have to offer which perhaps we value chiefly just because it is our own. Similarly we often yield to the impulse to enhance the glory of our gospel by insisting that all men need salvation when perhaps only some of them do.

The instinct is akin to that which is vulgarly known as salesmanship—we endeavour in the interest of what we have to sell to create a need where it does not already exist. I do not mean to suggest that the belief that all men are sinners and in need of a supernatural salvation arose from such an instinct; Paul got the belief from the Hellenistic philosophy of his day interpreted in the light of his own experience, and it was from him that it entered the thought of the church. But without doubt its prevalence has been promoted by the recognition of the heightened value it gives to the Christian gospel. No one has ever proved that all men need salvation; it is, of course, a mere hypothesis. The words of Jesus, "Not they that are whole need a physician but they that are sick," suggest a different attitude. Evidently, as I have already said, Catholic exclusiveness easily lends itself to abuse, but even so it has sprung from a wholesome instinct and is not to be condemned without discrimination.

In Catholic history there has been a constant struggle between the two principles of inclusiveness and exclusiveness, the one positive, the other negative. And yet as apprehended by Catholics themselves they are not two principles but one. Catholicism has always claimed to be coextensive with Christianity and hence has striven to include everything Christian. But not everything is Christian that claims to be and hence the lines have been drawn not between Catholic and non-Catholic Christianity (the latter a fiction only), but between the Christian and the non-Christian. It is not the Catholic's definition of Catholicism that is too narrow but his definition of Christianity.

There have been periods when the Catholic claim that Catholicism and Christianity are coextensive seemed fairly well supported by the facts, but there have been other periods, particularly since the sixteenth century, when it has run so patently counter to the facts as to seem absurd to a considerable part of the Christian world and for that matter even to certain Catholics themselves, for there have always been those within the Roman communion who believe salvation possible outside the papal establishment.[9] But they have been exceptional. To most Catholics such breadth has seemed a betrayal of the faith.

Since the inclusiveness aimed at by Catholicism is not unlimited, but is confined to what is Christian, it has exclusiveness as its inevitable accompaniment, and this however broad its platform in comparison with the platforms of the sects. As a matter of fact its platform has sometimes been very broad as was the case during much of the Middle Ages when its ascendancy gave it the serenity of strength. Again it has grown narrow when in the face of criticism and contradiction confidence has given way to fear. Only thus can we explain the Council of Trent—the answer of the Catholic church to the Protestant Reformation—and the attitude of Pius X and the curia toward the Catholic modernism of a few years ago.

[9] Cf. von Hügel: Essays and Addresses on the Philosophy of Religion, 1st Series, pp. 234 f.

Inclusiveness and exclusiveness are but two inseparable aspects of the one faith that Catholicism and Christianity are synonymous. Because Catholicism counts itself synonymous with Christianity it aims to include everything that is Christian and to exclude everything that is not. Whether at any particular time the former or the latter aim predominates depends not on the genius of the Catholic church but on the situation in which it finds itself and on the character of those who direct its destinies.

Chapter IV

PROTESTANTISM

In spite of all the Roman Catholic church was doing for its members discontent with it was spreading rapidly in the late Middle Ages. Its dominance in the affairs of the world was opposed in the interest both of secularism and of nationalism. The financial exactions of the curia were breeding resentment and its worldly aims were alienating many. The teachings of the church, particularly as formulated by the later schoolmen, seemed artificial and far-removed from the simplicity of the gospel; in its conservatism it was too little sympathetic with the ideas and ideals of a period of ferment and change; its institutionalism was cramping the growing spirit of individualism and independence; true religion, the communion of the soul with God, was finding itself distracted by rites and ceremonies, and true virtue, the service of one's fellows in the spirit of Jesus Christ, was finding itself hindered by multiform religious duties. Mystics and humanists alike, though on very different grounds, were becoming impatient and wishing for a change. Multitudes, both religious and irreligious, would have been glad to break with the ecclesiastical establishment if they had dared; but there was nothing to take its place—no other institution in which they could find eternal salvation—and so they retained their connection with it and availed themselves of its ministrations even when they were largely out of sympathy with it. The grounds of their growing disaffection were many and various—political, economic, intellectual, ethical, religious, theological—and were sometimes creditable, sometimes discreditable. In any event to renounce the one ark of salvation was for most men—cultured or ignorant, theologian or layman, ruler or subject—quite impossible. The extraordinary thing about Martin Luther was that he succeeded in convincing large numbers of his contemporaries that salvation was to be had outside the church of their fathers and thus opened the way for their wholesale desertion of it. How he succeeded in doing this is a marvel, almost as great a marvel as the continuance among Jesus' disciples of the belief in his Messiahship when he died without doing Messiah's work. To convince half the western world that the Roman Catholic church was not what it claimed to be, not what it had been generally believed to be for a thousand years, the alone ark of salvation and the supreme authority upon earth, but that truth and salvation were actually to be found in another institution altogether—this was an achievement hardly to be matched in human history. Only a man of commanding personality, of deep religious conviction, of transparent sincerity, of matchless insight into the human heart and of extraordinary polemic gifts, could have done what he did. Probably few of those who were influenced by Luther shared his difficulties or really understood his gospel, but they had reason enough, as has been seen, for desiring some change and when they became satisfied that it was safe to follow him they did so in immense numbers.

The Reformation is often spoken of as a modern movement, as if it were the fruit of the new intellectual forces at work in humanism and represented the spirit of enlightenment as compared with the church of the Middle Ages. Nothing could be farther from the truth. Luther was a mediævalist not a modernist. He had no intellectual difficulties with the traditional system and was as superstitious and credulous as the extremest of Catholics. The contrast between him and Erasmus is illuminating. The latter was far more modern than Luther in his mental attitudes and far more critical of mediæval obscurantism, but he remained within the old church and that not from unworthy motives, as is often alleged, but because he believed, as many others did, that intellectual progress would be impeded rather than forwarded by Luther's movement. That a man of Erasmus' acumen and unparalleled acquaintance with Catholicism past and present could believe that the reformation desired by him and many other humanists was possible within the existing establishment—a reformation involving not only change and improvement in details but a radical simplification of the traditional system in the interest both of religion and ethics—is a very significant fact. It shows that Roman Catholicism in the sixteenth century was not as rigid and stereotyped as we are apt to imagine.

It is not surprising that Luther, much less radical in

temper than Erasmus, should believe himself a sound Catholic and for some time after he got in conflict with the authorities should expect to be allowed to stay in the church of his fathers and carry on his work within it. There were enough who were delighted to leave the church when the opportunity came but he was not of their number. He went out only when he was compelled to and only when he was convinced not merely that salvation was possible outside the existing establishment but that it was no longer possible within it.

His conviction that salvation was possible outside the existing establishment was due to his own searching religious experience. Driven by fear of the divine wrath into a monastery and asceticism of an extreme type, he finally found the effort to appease God by penitential practices wholly vain and was led to throw himself completely upon the love of God in Christ for the forgiveness he could not do without. In the peace that ensued—a peace known by many devout souls in every age—he came to recognize the salvation he sought. Thenceforth the gospel of a present salvation through faith alone was the most precious thing in the world to him and the effort to win the favour of God by meritorious works of any kind seemed not only vain but profane and antichristian. For some years he supposed his gospel was in accord with the teachings of the Catholic church; he had found it he thought both in Paul and Augustine, and his knowledge of church history was very slender. Only gradually did his mistake become clear to him. Even then he strove to secure if not the acceptance at least the tolerance of his gospel by the ecclesiastical authorities, but when they condemned it as heretical and pronounced him excommunicate unless he would recant there was nothing for him to do but to take his gospel with him and be gone. The attitude of the Roman hierarchy convinced him finally that the Pope was Antichrist and his church antichristian. To leave it was therefore imperative for all true Christians. Thenceforth his life was devoted to two tasks: to convince his contemporaries that if they would be saved they must flee the old church, and to provide another church in which they could find the salvation no longer to be had there.

It was far from Luther's thought to do away with the church altogether. On the contrary he insisted that the church is "the mother of those that believe," is absolutely necessary to salvation, not to be sure, as the Catholics maintained, because in it alone is sacramental grace to be had, but because in it alone is proclaimed the gospel of God's forgiving love in Christ without which no one can believe unto salvation. It was therefore not a particular ecclesiastical institution, the papal or any other, that Luther had in mind when he spoke of the church, but the company of Christian believers who alone know and can proclaim the gospel. Wherever the gospel of God's forgiving love in Christ and salvation through faith in him are proclaimed there is the true church and there is the word of God which is its one indispensable mark and guarantee. The sacraments he also spoke of as marks of the true church, but this was only because in them he saw the word made visible, the gospel of God's forgiving love in Christ set forth in external form. It was for this reason that he reduced the number of sacraments from seven to three (baptism, penance, and the eucharist) and finally to two (baptism and the eucharist). These alone he believed bore witness to the gospel of God's forgiving love in Christ and thus fulfilled the true function of a sacrament. It was no mere negative task that Luther undertook—to deliver men from the Catholic church —but the positive task of putting something in its place to mediate life and salvation and to meet the spiritual needs which the old church had met for many centuries.

Among those needs the primary one in Luther's thinking was reconciliation with God and the peace that comes from the knowledge of his forgiving love. This was met adequately as he believed by the preaching of the gospel, fortified by the sacraments, its visible signs. To attempt to earn it by works of penance or to purchase it by the sacrifice of the mass was to forfeit it altogether. A hierarchy was no longer needed and sacerdotalism went by the board. All Christians are priests and have immediate access to God in Christ.

There would seem on these principles to be no place left for clergymen, but Luther realized that his new churches must be organized if they were to maintain themselves, that the people needed guidance under the new system as under the old, and that the regular proclamation of the gospel and administration of the sacraments, its visible signs and seals, must be provided for; and so the new church had its clergy and its laity like the old. But whereas the chief function of the Catholic clergyman was to administer the sacraments the chief function of the evangelical clergyman was to preach the word. For the former ordination was the essential prerequisite, for the latter education.

Another need always prominent within Catholicism was the need so keenly felt by Paul, of divine power to enable a man to live as God would have him live. By nature corrupt and incapable of holiness, as he was generally believed to be, he must have supernatural aid if he were to resist and overcome his inborn tendency to sin. To meet this need was one of the functions of the sacraments through which alone the indispensable divine grace could be secured. According to Luther nothing of the sort is required. Saving faith is itself impulse and power to Christian living and needs no supplementing from without. Christian living is nothing else than the service of one's fellows in disinterested love. Set free from fear and from anxiety about his own salvation the Christian believer, who is already a saved man, is in a position to give himself unreservedly to his brothers' good as his Christian faith inevitably prompts him to do. Faith was thus a creative power as Luther understood it; not mere passive receptivity but active devotion. Experience shows, however, that this is one of the most difficult conceptions in the whole range of theology. Almost invariably something more than mere faith is felt to be necessary if a man, conscious of his sinfulness, is to live as he ought to live. This is particularly the case when faith comes to mean, as it almost inevitably does and as it early did in the Protestant church, the acceptance of sound doctrine, thus losing immediate religious and ethical significance. Even Luther himself was not always consistent and while he never fell back into the Catholic way of talking about divine grace as needed to supplement human effort, he did talk in Pauline fashion about the Holy Spirit dwelling in the hearts of believers and sanctifying and empowering them; and the difference is more verbal than real. Luther might maintain, as his followers did after him, the doctrine of justification by faith alone, but sanctification was recognized as the work of the Spirit and so the ancient need of superhuman power to enable a man to live in holiness and righteousness was met much in the old way. Even the sacramental aspect of the matter was retained, for in spite of Luther's insistence that the sacraments are only visible signs of the gospel of God's forgiving love in Christ, they came to be thought of both in the Lutheran and Calvinistic wings of the church (and not without warrant from Luther himself) as means of becoming united to Christ and feeding on him. Thus Protestantism met the historic need of divine power as effectively for Protestants as Catholicism did for Catholics. Protestantism did not mean the disappearance of the need but the satisfaction of it in a different though no less supernatural way.

Another need met by Catholicism was that of an infallible authority on which to rely in all matters having to do with salvation. This need also Protestantism met in a manner satisfactory to its adherents. Luther appealed from the Pope ill-informed to the Pope to-be-better-informed, then from Pope to Council and finally from Council to Bible—the resort of many others before him who found themselves out of agreement with the church. And though Luther himself distinguished between the Bible and the word of God, or the gospel of God's forgiving love in Christ, and made the latter fundamental rather than the former, in the controversy with Romanists on the one side and radicals on the other he frequently lost sight of the distinction and the Bible became for him and still more for his followers the ultimate authority in all matters of doctrine and morals and in the Reformed wing of Protestantism, in government and discipline as well. It was appealed to by Protestants with the same confidence as the authority of the church by Catholics. Thus the historic need of infallibility was met in another way to be sure but in a way not essentially different from the old. The Bible taken by itself was as final and unquestioned an authority as the church had ever been. Because the Bible may be interpreted in many different ways some have found it a less satisfying authority than the Roman church which claims infallibility for its particular interpretation of the Bible; and hence Protestants who feel the need of an infallible interpreter sometimes take refuge in the Roman communion. But this should not blind us to the fact that multitudes find their need of an infallible authority adequately met by the Bible interpreted by themselves or by their sect and thus have all the assurance that any Catholic enjoys.

In one respect indeed the Protestant has a great advantage over the Romanist for his faith gives him the assurance of salvation to which the Catholic cannot hope to aspire. Upon this Luther laid the greatest stress. Above all else he was concerned to do away with the fear and anxiety for one's own fate which led to penitential works and prevented, so he believed, the disinterested and single-minded service of one's fellows. According to Catholic theory such fear and anxiety are needed to keep men—naturally depraved and indolent as they are—from relaxing their efforts and falling into sin. Salvation is to be attained only by a lifetime of struggle; premature assurance of it is both presumptuous and dangerous. At this point Luther was diametrically opposed to Catholic theory and practice and his doctrine of assurance undoubtedly proved a great strength to Protestantism. Unfortunately it easily degenerated into spiritual pride and often had the ill effects the Catholics ascribed to it; and it was too much out of line with common human experience to maintain itself in the consciousness of the average Protestant. With it was lost that controlling sense of salvation as a present reality upon which Protestantism as a distinctive form of Christianity was really built.

In the previous chapter it was said that one of the characteristic marks of Catholicism is the sense of antiquity and continuity. Though Protestantism broke with Catholicism and pronounced the Middle Ages a period of apostasy from the true gospel it claimed to be a return to the pure Christianity of an earlier age and thus maintained the note of antiquity as zealously as Catholicism itself. And the Reformers were not altogether wrong in this claim. As a matter of fact Protestantism was an ancient not a modern thing, thoroughly at one in most respects with the Apostles and the Fathers. To be sure the gospel of salvation through faith alone and the principle of Christian liberty of which Luther made so much were rare in any age, and were more of a novelty than Luther himself realized. But that is neither here nor there. The point I wish to make is that by his appeal to Paul and his insistence that Protestantism represented primitive Christianity in contrast with the mediævalism of Catholicism, Luther met the traditional desire for antiquity even though he recognized that continuity had been broken and had to be re-established by going back again to the original springs. His attitude shows clearly enough that he too needed external authority in religion and the support of the experience and faith of other Christians.

One note of Catholicism the Protestants could lay no claim to, at least no just claim, the note of unity. In setting up another church apart from the Roman Catholic establishment Luther deliberately destroyed the unity of western Christendom. In doing so he sacrificed what seemed to him the lesser interest to the greater; but it is significant that he counted something else more important than unity, for he thus broke with the age-long conviction of the Catholic church. Since the time of Cyprian unity had been esteemed an indispensable mark of the true church; to destroy the unity of the church was to destroy the church itself. Despite its own separation from the Greek church the Roman church gloried in its unity and found in it nourishment for Christian experience of a very deep and vital kind. Not only by breaking with Catholicism, but by rejecting all Christian fellowship with Zwingli and his followers, Luther showed clearly enough that in spite of what he said about the unity of the true church, the one church of Christ, he yet counted unity a relatively minor matter, and the same is true of those who came after him. Unity in the sense of fellowship with those of like mind and faith continued to be valued; but in the larger sense of a universal brotherhood, of an institution embracing all the earth, it never got a foothold in Protestantism. The particular kind of religious exaltation that comes from this sense of universality has therefore been generally lacking in Protestantism and is one of the chief defects felt by genuine Catholics in their estimate of it. There is a widespread effort in our own day to recover the lost unity by overcoming the countless divisions in the ranks of Protestantism, but Protestants have lived so long without unity that it seems to most of them an artificial thing and considerable effort is required even to arouse a languid interest in it. The contrast at this point between the Protestant and Catholic world is very striking. I am inclined to think that in the feeling for unity and universality or in the lack of it the difference between Catholicism and Protestantism reveals itself most clearly.

The counterpart of unity and universality, as seen in the previous chapter, is exclusiveness. Catholicism is not simply an inclusive but an exclusive thing, and here Protestantism and Catholicism are akin. As already remarked, in breaking with the Catholic church Luther asserted not only that salvation is possible apart from it, but that it is not the true church and must be abandoned if one would be saved. This of course meant an exclusiveness as extreme as that of Catholicism, and it meant also that Protestants found in their new church all the religious satisfactions that such exclusiveness is fitted to produce: the pride of being God's peculiar people, the sense of superiority to others, the conviction that one is called to convert one's fellows and bring them within the saving pale. All the good and evil of religious exclusiveness belonged to Protestantism as well as to Catholicism. But in Protestantism it lacked a certain largeness and breadth which marked Catholicism, for the exclusiveness was no longer that of a world-wide or continent-wide institution which with some show of justice could claim to be the repository of all the Christianity there was in the western hemisphere. The exclusiveness of Protestantism like that of primitive Christianity was the exclusiveness of a minority, particularly when it meant as it early came to mean the exclusion from the household of faith not only of Roman Catholics but of other Protestant bodies as well. The sectarianism of Protestantism is much

uglier than that of Catholicism, for the smaller the body
that makes the claim to be the true church, the greater
the presumption, and the less important the differences
that separate it from others, the pettier the attitude.
The Catholics are justified in regarding sectarianism as
one of the gravest counts in their indictment against
Protestantism, and that too even though it represents
no other principle than finds expression in Catholicism
itself.

In another respect Protestant sectarianism is worse
than Catholic for it has its roots in intellectual differences or in variety of doctrine. Because Zwingli held
another view of the Lord's Supper Luther refused to
count him a Christian brother, and because Calvinists
and Arminians differed on the doctrine of predestina-
tion they could not remain in the same communion. In
this respect Catholicism has held a different attitude.
It has admitted the legitimacy of large variety in
thought and belief and has been willing to tolerate
within its capacious fold all that recognize its authority
and submit to its discipline. It has never excommunicated any one simply for holding opinions different
from its own, but for promulgating them in defiance of
the express prohibition of the church; in other words
the real ground of condemnation has been contumacy,
not heresy. Protestantism has demanded intellectual
agreement, Catholicism a certain temper and attitude.
There can be no doubt that the former is farther removed from the genius of Christianity as an ethical
religion than the latter. It is true that Catholic eccle-

siasticism represents a serious departure from the teaching of Jesus, but it is no more alien to his spirit than the traditional Protestant belief that theological agreement is essential to Christian fellowship.

Another need met by Catholic Christianity was the common religious need of communion with God. To this Protestantism also ministered; had it not it could never have supplanted Catholicism as it did. Communion with God is possible in all sorts of circumstances and under all sorts of conditions. It may be had within an ecclesiastical institution and by the use of means regularly appointed thereto; it may be had in public services of worship and in association with other worshippers; or it may be had apart and alone without the use of aids or media of any kind. It cannot be bound by rules or limited to certain forms and ceremonies or confined to particular times and places. Catholicism has always recognized this and has granted the widest latitude for the converse of the devout soul with the divine. The formalist and the legalist and the mystic have found themselves equally at home within the Roman communion. This has been one of the chief sources of its strength. A world religion it could never have become on any narrower terms. But Catholicism has no advantage over Protestantism in this matter. Many have thought it has. Luther's repudiation of sacramentarianism, sacerdotalism, and asceticism has led to the supposition that Protestantism ministers only to a particular kind of temperament and meets only a particular type of religious need. Nothing could be farther

from the truth. Were Catholicism divided from Protestantism in any such way the religious situation in
western Christendom would be much less complicated
than it is. Protestantism is not made up simply of those
who have deliberately chosen it in contrast with Catholicism. For the most part men are born Protestants just
as they are born Catholics, and that they are Protestants
rather than Catholics is no guarantee that they will not
feel the common religious needs that Catholics too feel.
Did they not find these needs met more or less adequately within their own communion, there would be
far more travelling back and forth than there actually is.[1]

A striking evidence of this is to be found in the matter of asceticism. It would seem as if in view of Luther's
attitude asceticism could find no home in Protestantism, and yet we read in Calvin the following striking
words: "He who commands us to use this world as
though we used it not, prohibits not only all intemperance in eating and drinking, and excessive delicacy,
ambition, pride, haughtiness and fastidiousness in our
furniture, our habitations and our apparel, but every

---

[1] Catholics are often deceived in supposing that the values they find in Catholicism are due to Catholicism as such, when they are perhaps due simply to the
fact that Catholicism is a religion and these values would be found equally in
all religions. Protestants often find every value in Protestantism that Catholics
find in Catholicism. The lack of unity is the most patent defect in Protestantism,
but that is not as a rule a serious thing and is rather theoretical than practical.
In communion with fellow members of the same church one finds usually all the
religious satisfaction one finds in communing in imagination with Christians in
all parts of the world. It is often said that it means much to the Catholic travel-
ler to find the same forms and the same language in every Catholic country.
But the Protestant often feels as much at home as he goes into a Protestant
service abroad. The attitude and general spirit are the same as at home and the
mere difference in forms to the average non-liturgical Protestant counts for little.

care and affection which would either seduce or disturb us from thoughts of the heavenly life and attention to the improvement of our souls."[2]

As a matter of fact while asceticism as a rule has not taken the extreme forms in Protestantism that have characterized it in Catholicism, and while it has never been so controlling, it has had a large place in the life of Protestant Christendom. To keep oneself unspotted from the world, to eschew worldly pleasures and employments, to subject the body to rigid discipline, to crucify the desires of the flesh, all for religion's sake—this has been the effort of multitudes of Protestants as well as Catholics. What is Puritanism indeed but a form of asceticism of a somewhat extreme type? Whether for good or ill asceticism is no monopoly of Catholic Christendom.[3]

Similarly with probation. In spite of Luther's theory that the believer is already a saved man through faith alone, the common religious experience that goes with the doctrine of probation early found a home in Protestantism, and though works of penance are theoretically repudiated as a superstition, many Protestants like their Catholic brethren hope that their good deeds will be counted to their credit at the judgment day. The very persistence in Protestant circles of the belief in a final judgment is proof enough of the continuance of the notion of probation, for it cannot be supposed

---

[2] *Institutes,* Bk. III, chap. 10, §4. See further, McGiffert, *Protestant Thought Before Kant,* pp. 91 *f.*

[3] It is interesting to note that extreme Protestantism at the farthest remove from Catholicism—Calvinism, Puritanism—is yet nearest Catholicism in principle at some points; *e.g.,* it makes more of external authority, of asceticism, of the Christian life as obedience to law and much less of Christian liberty.

that the artificial interpretation of the judgment as a mere spectacle which orthodox Protestant theology is obliged to insist upon is shared by the Protestant rank and file.

I have been speaking of Catholicism and Protestantism as a whole. It cannot be denied that Protestant sects are somewhat differently related to one another. Sometimes they have been based on differences in religious need and temperament, and migrations from one Protestant sect to another have therefore been more numerous than migrations from Protestantism to Catholicism and the reverse. But as a rule in course of time each denomination has become in turn the home of the most diverse temperaments and has met the widest variety of religious needs. It may have made more of some needs than of others, and it may have met these in its own way, but commonly there has been room within it for a large variety of temperament and experience.

What I have been saying about the identity of religious needs in Catholicism and Protestantism holds true also, though in somewhat lesser measure, of religious beliefs. Theologically as well as practically Protestantism is largely at one with Catholicism. This is not surprising, for Protestantism was not a protest against the Catholic system as a whole but only against certain features of it. Thus orthodox Protestantism agrees with Catholicism that all men are corrupt and depraved and helpless and will inevitably suffer eternal punishment unless saved by supernatural means;

that all men are blind and can know the way of salvation only as it is supernaturally revealed; that God is a god of wrath and is made gracious only by the work of Christ who is at once God and man, the second person of the Trinity, the pre-existent Son of God, incarnate, dead, risen, and ascended. Orthodox Protestantism accepts also the divine inspiration and authority of the Bible and hence many things recorded in it which have no immediate connection with the doctrine of salvation, such as creation in six days, miracles, the virgin birth, the second coming of Christ. It believes, too, like Catholicism, in the presence and power of the Holy Spirit, in the supernatural origin and guidance of the church, and in the sacraments as means of grace; and all its thinking moves in the common traditional framework of the old dualism between matter and spirit, nature and the supernatural, earth and heaven, the human and the divine. In all these respects orthodox Protestantism and orthodox Catholicism are identical. Compared with these identities the differences are but minor and concern chiefly the doctrine of the church or not so much the doctrine of the church as its identity.

Other doctrines in which they differ are less fundamental than the agreements, yet they have great significance. These differences have to do with objects of worship and the like and may be schematized as follows, in each case the Catholic position being given first:

Objects of worship:

    Mary and the saints

    God and Christ and Spirit alone

Methods of worship:
  Ceremonies, saints' days, etc.
  Relative freedom but approaching
    Catholic ceremonies

Way of salvation:
  Church, the ark of salvation
  Church, the community of the saved

  Church has absolute authority
  Church has relative authority

  Salvation by faith and works and sacraments
  Salvation by faith alone

  Sacraments, means of imparting grace
  Sacraments, signs of the Word

  The Christian, a candidate for salvation
  The Christian, a saved man

Belief (for Catholic layman) implicit only: "I
  believe all that the holy Catholic church commands me to believe." Duty to știfle all doubts
  as though they were unclean thoughts. The
  same is true with the moral law. It is to be
  obeyed because the church commands it. Catholic ethic protects particularly marriage and
  property. The Catholic priest must have explicit belief also.
Belief (for Protestant layman) explicit: "I believe the several articles of the creed," or "ac-

cept Christ." Doctrinal content more important than in Catholicism for the church is less important. Protestantism demands a harder thing than Catholicism, that is, actual acceptance, *free* belief: a question not of obedience but of religious or philosophical truth.

It still remains true, however, that the great difference between Catholics and Protestants is that the former belong to a particular institution ruled over by the Pope, the vicar of Christ, while Protestants of every sect are without its pale.

CHAPTER V

MODERNISM

Modernism is a vague word and in this chapter I shall employ it in a vague sense to cover attitudes and beliefs contrasted more or less sharply with those that characterized primitive Christianity, Catholicism, and Protestantism, as described in the previous chapters. Attitudes that might fairly have been called modernist have existed in every age; every age is modern to those that dwell in it; and in every age there are some that are conscious of their differences with the Fathers. But in recent generations such attitudes have found a larger place within the Christian church than in other days, and have become so important and so widely prevalent as to demand separate consideration. My concern in this chapter is not with those outside the Christian church, or with those who have broken with organized Christianity altogether, either because they are indifferent to religion or because the church fails to meet their ideals or satisfy their needs. I am interested here in modernism as a form of Christianity, distinct in many respects from the Christianity of the past and yet counting itself truly Christian and maintaining its right to a place within the church of Christ.

Modernism is not an organized movement and has not ordinarily led to the formation of independent sects. It represents rather an attitude or frame of mind or way of looking at things that appears in most of our Protestant communions. It is found even within Roman Catholicism but there, owing to its background and environment, it is so different in some important respects from Protestant modernism that I shall not try to include it here.[1]

Because modernism is unorganized and represents rather an attitude or frame of mind than a particular creed or a definite program it is exceedingly difficult to compass and define. Indeed it eludes definition altogether, for it is protean in form and is constantly developing and changing. Nevertheless there is such a thing as modernism and it is possible for all its vagueness and variety to distinguish it more or less sharply from traditional Christianity, both Catholic and Protestant.

In speaking of Catholicism and Protestantism I have had a good deal to say about human needs and their satisfaction. Let us consider modernism from the same point of view. Both Catholicism and Protestantism meet certain religious needs that for centuries have been widely felt in the western world. What we know as modernism has become prevalent in modern times partly because these needs are less generally and less keenly felt than they once were, and partly because new needs not met by the older forms of Christianity have emerged and are clamouring for satisfaction. To the

[1] I have dealt with this subject in a Dudleian lecture given at the Harvard Divinity School and published in the *Harvard Theological Review* for January, 1910.

modernist the old system is uncongenial not only because it ministers to needs which he has outgrown but also because it fails to minister to needs which are vital to him. The latter from the modernist's point of view is the graver defect. He might feel still at home in the old even though much of it served ends which were not his, if he could only find his own needs adequately met by it. Let us consider first this more vital aspect of the matter. What are some of the needs of the modern Christian which the traditional system fails to satisfy?

For one thing the development of modern science has given birth to a need not felt—or at any rate not felt to the same degree—in any other period of Christian history: the need of such an interpretation of the world as shall make religious faith possible to the man who believes in the scientific method and accepts the results of scientific observation and experiment.

At many points the teachings of modern science on the one hand and of the Bible and the church on the other are diametrically opposed. As a consequence some —known commonly today as fundamentalists—reject the findings of science in the interest of what they count Christianity; some reject Christianity in the interest of science and are to be found outside of our churches altogether; while some, whom we may call modernists, believing both in science and in Christianity, are driven to find some way of reconciling the seemingly irreconcilable. As long as the prevailing science of the day agreed with the Bible and the church this need of reconciliation did not exist, but in our modern world in which the disagreement is so marked the need has become very pressing. Father Tyrrell defines modernism in the following terms: "The hope of a synthesis between the essentials of Christianity and the assured results of criticism is very widespread nowadays, and those who share it are commonly called Modernists, or Liberals. There is a marked division of Modernists according as their tendency is to consider that alone to be essential to Christianity which agrees with their idea of the assured results of criticism, or to consider as the only assured results of criticism those that fit in with their conception of the essentials of Christianity. Both tendencies are vicious and, if unchecked, destroy the very idea of Modernism which professes to consider each interest impartially, without respect to the other, in the belief and hope that the results will prove harmonious."[2] According to this definition, and I know no better one, the man who turns his back on science is not a modernist, nor the man who turns his back on religion, but the man who accepts them both and among whose religious needs therefore is the need of adjusting the one to the other.

I have already called attention to the success with which Catholicism and traditional Protestantism met certain great religious needs. The success with which modernism has met this new religious need is no less signal and complete. It is not merely that modernism has reconciled religion with the science of today, showing that

[2] George Tyrrell, *Christianity at the Cross-Roads*, p. xv.

the particular results reached in one or another field of experiment and discovery, physics, chemistry, biology and what not are consistent with belief in Christianity. It has done much more than this for it has removed all possibility of conflict between Christianity and the science of any future age. Fundamentalists often taunt modernists with the futility of striving to reconcile religion with scientific discoveries which may shortly be proved erroneous—as such discoveries frequently are. And if this were all modernists were doing the taunt would be fully justified. But modernism is actually doing something much more important and enduring. No doubt religious men have frequently contented themselves with squaring their religious faith with some scientific discovery or theory and have then had to go through the process again with the same labor and anxiety when new discoveries and theories approved themselves as sound. But this is no adequate reconciliation of religion and science and it is not the kind of thing I am talking about. Indeed it may not even deserve the name of modernism at all. After much hesitation and heartburning the church, both Catholic and Protestant, finally adjusted itself to the Copernican astronomy without therefore becoming a modernist church. In a similar way it will ultimately adjust itself to evolution without necessarily becoming any more modernist in spirit than it is now, for it will probably still go on distrusting science and opposing its development as bitterly as heretofore.

The modernism of which I am speaking is something

altogether different. It makes such repeated adjust-
ments between religion and science quite unnecessary.
It gives the religious man a new point of view so that he
is lifted above all fear and anxiety and can face the de-
velopments of science not merely with equanimity but
with the same interest and satisfaction that any other
man may feel. For what has happened is not that religion has been disentangled from the particular scientific beliefs of Biblical writers and mediæval theologians
in order to be tied up with the scientific beliefs of the
twentieth century, but that it has come to be recognized as another thing than science altogether, equally
at home with any scientific fact or theory, as goodness is,
or love, or devotion, or the sense of beauty, or the desire
for happiness. It has come to be recognized that as
Christianity is not identical with any particular metaphysics, so it is not identical with any particular physics,
that it is a matter of worship and inspiration and service. It is a great pity that faith in God early got tied
up with the Hebrew cosmogony, so that a man was supposed to be an atheist if he did not believe that God
created the world in the way described in the book of
Genesis. The modernist knows that a man may still
believe in God though he reads the ancient creation story
as mere poetry or rejects it altogether. For that matter he knows that a man may believe in God without believing in any doctrine of divine creation whatsoever.
He may for instance believe in the immanence of God
and read all the phenomena of nature as ways in which
God works. In other words he may interpret the uni-

verse theistically and no scientist can possibly say him nay. All nature to such a believer is instinct with the divine, and nature and the supernatural are not two realms but one. To such a believer everything is natural and supernatural at once. He finds God in the commonest facts of everyday life and not alone in signs and wonders. Science is thus given its full rights and its explanation of natural phenomena is accepted without demur; but a new interpretation is put upon them all, not to the impoverishment of science but to the enrichment of life.[3]

Or it may be that the modernist following the line of theistic development turns from the world of nature to find God in another realm, the realm of moral purpose.[4] In either case whether he be more interested in divine immanence or in a righteous God working out his good purposes and building his kingdom of mutual love and sympathy and service among men, the modernist finds the old conflict between science and religion wholly transcended and thus one of the crying religious needs of modern times adequately and permanently satisfied.

Another pressing religious need of our day is the need of finding God in social service. The development in modern times of the social conscience and the growth of interest in the welfare of humanity and in the improvement of the institutions of society and of the conditions under which men live have led to a readjustment of traditional religious values so that the old orthodoxy no longer meets the needs of the new age. The salva-

3 See McGiffert, *The Rise of Modern Religious Ideas,* pp. 179, 204.
4 See *ibid.,* pp. 226 *ff.*

tion of one's own soul—for which the old system chiefly provided—has ceased to be the dominant interest of a growing multitude of men and women and its place has been taken by a new concern, not for the salvation of other people's souls but for their health and happiness and prosperity. There is perhaps as much selfishness and self-seeking in the world today as there ever was, but it is a fact that in the minds of the best men of our age the social virtues overshadow the self-regarding virtues to a degree never seen before in Christian history. It is inevitable that this should have its effect in the religious sphere, that religious men should be driven to find God in social service rather than in asceticism and the solitary life. Catholicism and much of Protestantism as well, for instance Puritanism, in which the traditional ascetic principle has found genuine though modified expression, are built upon the assumption of the corruptness and depravity of man and the evil and impermanence of the world. To find God you must turn your back on your fellows and seek him in quietness and solitude or you must eschew certain worldly employments and occupations and discover him through self-denial and repression. Modernists do not deny that God may thus be found; many of them recognize the religious value of the old ways. But they are not satisfied to leave an ever enlarging realm of human interest and endeavour devoid of religious value and significance, or to reduce it to a mere item in the duty of Christian men. They feel the need of enlarging the conception of the divine and multiplying the ways of access to God.

Not in Christ alone is God incarnate but in the lives of men and women everywhere, and not alone by the sacraments or by the worship of the church or by prayer and contemplation is he to be found but by the service of one's fellows and by earnest and resolute toil at the building of the kingdom of mutual love and sympathy and brotherliness among men.

This means not simply the emergence of a new need but the discovery of a new way of meeting an old need, the need of communion or fellowship with the divine. A standing religious need this is; and one of the difficulties with the old system felt by many a modern man is the way in which it has narrowed and circumscribed the paths that lead to God. A greater catholicity in this matter is of the essence of what we know as modernism. The modernist is instinctively hospitable to other experiences and other ways of thinking than his own and he rejoices when men find God as he believes they may truly find him, not only in the visible church Catholic or Protestant but in other religions altogether and apart from all organized and formal religion, in science, in art, in social service, in strenuous and self-forgetting achievement of any sort.

A new interpretation of religion—broader, more humane and if you will more secular; a new interpretation of the world, more sympathetic and more spiritual; a new interpretation of humanity, more charitable, more idealistic and more trustful—all this I think we may fairly say is characteristic of the modernism of our day.

Closely related to the need I have just been speaking of is the need of finding religious value in man's present life. As a result of various influences which I cannot stop to consider here the present world has come to occupy a larger place in the thought of religious men than it once did. Christian tradition contrasts the present world and the present life of men to their great disadvantage with another world and a future life beyond the grave. The present world and the earthly life of man are but temporary and are beset with evil and corruption. Satan is the god of this world according to St. Paul, who set the fashion for all the centuries to follow, and in his present life man is subject to the lusts of the flesh and the temptations of the world and the devil. In contrast with all this there is another world where the redeemed will enjoy an eternal life of uninterrupted holiness and bliss.

This contrast which controlled the life and thought of the Christian church for many centuries and is still widely influential has lost something of its significance for the modernist. This does not mean that modernists have ceased to believe in a future life. Many of them believe in it as truly as the Fathers did.[5] Indeed it would be wholly unjust to modernism to tax it with the loss of such belief. But it does mean that the present world and the present life bulk more largely and that immortality is less controlling in the thought of the modernist than in traditional Christianity. The religion of the average modernist is without question primarily,

[5] See, for instance, W. A. Brown, *The Christian Hope;* and H. E. Fosdick, *The Assurance of Immortality.*

though by no means exclusively, a this-worldly religion. By which I mean that it is its value for this world and its influence upon this life that seem chiefly important. Christianity is a true and good religion not if it saves men's souls for heaven and fits them for life there, but if it brings them into communion with God here, makes them more conscious of his presence and more responsive to his will and transforms them into better citizens of this world—better husbands, fathers, neighbours, employers. The modernist insists that religions like men must be judged by their fruits rather than by their promises and he finds in the fruits of Christianity its guarantee.

All this means not the minimizing of another world but the magnifying of this and it creates a religious need not wholly new, for it has been felt by many both pagan and Christian in all the centuries, but generally unrecognized in traditional Catholicism and Protestantism. The need is to find religious value and meaning in the present life and in the present world—to remove them from the category of the unworthy and unholy and profane and make them part and parcel of the divine and eternal. This has found expression again in the doctrine of divine immanence and in the conception of the present world as the scene of the kingdom of God.

Eternal life has come to have among modernists qualitative rather than temporal connotation—the immediate consciousness of God even now and here as Schleiermacher defined it, or victory over the world in devotion to the progress of God's kingdom in the earth as Ritschl defined it.

I have been speaking of certain religious needs felt particularly in modern times which are not met by traditional Christianity either Catholic or Protestant and have led modernists to feel the inadequacy of the old forms and conceptions. But modernists find those old forms and conceptions uncongenial also because they minister so largely to religious needs which the modernists have outgrown or have lost interest in.

In the second chapter I called attention to the fact that primitive Gentile Christianity was a religion of personal salvation—one of the many mystery-religions of the Roman Empire, but superior to all the others because of its Jewish heritage and its Lord Jesus Christ. Organized Christianity has never lost this note of personal salvation; whether in Catholicism or in Protestantism personal salvation has been the fundamental thing. It is characteristic of modernism that this interest in personal salvation bulks less largely than in traditional Christianity. Not that modernists are no longer interested in personal salvation; doubtless many of them are; but it has ceased to be central and dominant with them. To define the Christianity of the average modernist as a religion of personal salvation would be to miss its real significance.

For one thing modernists have ceased to believe in everlasting punishment. Not merely is their sense of justice outraged by it but the whole legalistic way of looking at God's relation to the world has come to seem artificial and unreal, and the conception of the future life as a place where rewards and punishments are to be meted out to those who have done well or ill in this life has largely faded out of their consciousness.[6] Similarly the old fear of divine wrath no longer troubles them as it troubled the Fathers.

Luther's great need was to find a gracious God. The need was not singular; it was felt by most devout and serious minded Catholics; but whereas the means offered by the Catholic system satisfied them they did not satisfy Luther. It seemed impossible for him to secure the favour of God in the ordinary way by penance and good works. And so he found another way—the way of faith in God's forgiving love in Christ.

The modernist is distinguished ordinarily both from Catholic and from orthodox Protestant by his lack of the need that pressed upon them. He has outgrown the traditional notion of God as a God of wrath and has come to think of him as essentially a God of love, who needs no propitiation either by Christ or by the Christian

---

[6] The old idea of immortality was either: a. Escape from death, i.e., personal survival. This was characteristic of the mystery-religions and of Paul. Paul's kinship with the mystery-religions is shown in his belief in the immortality of the saved only, not of others. b. Escape from future punishment. The latter is outstanding in Christianity. The interest in immortality in Christian history has not commonly been an interest in immortality at all, but in escape from sin. Not to be immortal but to escape punishment has been the kernel of the hope. This became common when immortality was expected for all, good and bad. And this is what belief in the future life has meant to most Christians. How was this idea lost? Partly by the development of a new imagination. In the old days the mind was fixed largely on the future and other world. In the modern age of discovery, invention, etc., the imagination has found play enough in *this* world and so has detached itself from a future and other world. Science, too, has undermined the old supernaturalism and with it the idea of divine sanctions of reward and punishment. Science has thrown everything into the framework of this world.

to make him gracious, and so the old doctrine of the atonement goes by the board as well as penance and saving grace.

Akin to this particular need is the need of divine forgiveness almost universally felt from the earliest days. It is characteristic of many modernists that they think little or not at all in terms of divine forgiveness. Sin is taken as a moral not a religious category: we sin against our fellows and may well desire their forgiveness, but our offenses against them are not offenses against God and do not need the divine forgiveness. No one can forgive sins, either God or man, except he against whom they are committed. To seek divine forgiveness for our ill treatment of our neighbours is to strive to ease our conscience without taking the only road appropriate thereto, the road of reparation and of reconciliation with the one injured.

In days when religious duties were recognized as distinct from moral duties, that is, duties toward God as distinct from duties toward one's fellows, there was reason in the desire for divine forgiveness. But ever since the Deistic controversy of the eighteenth century there has been a growing disinclination to think of religious duties as distinct from moral duties. Duty it is widely believed is an ethical not a religious category and has to do with our relations to our fellows, individually and collectively, and not with our relations to God. Our relation to God is a matter of privilege rather than duty or there are no duties to God apart from duties to men.

While it would be too much to say that all modernists take this attitude, there can be no doubt that it is common among them and that it is tending to sharpen the social conscience of many.

It is often said that to interpret every unrighteous act or every offense against one's fellows as an offense against God is to heighten the heinousness of it and thus quicken the reaction of the conscience against it. This has been the common Christian position during all the centuries, but it may well be doubted whether it is really so; whether reading our offenses against our fellows as offenses against God has not tended to make us lose sight of the evil consequences suffered by them and to content ourselves with securing reconciliation with God —ordinarily a much easier matter both because he is invisible and because there is no reparation he needs from us.

Similarly the old idea of an evil world from which we need to escape has given way to the idea of the world as a place of opportunity, as a plastic world which may be moulded to God's will and brought under the control of his spirit if we will but do our part in making him known to men. To turn one's back upon the world has come to seem to most modernists recreancy to their appointed task and the abandonment of their paramount duty. Doubtless the old eagerness to escape from death which was one of the interests underlying the development of the mystery-religions in the ancient world is still shared by many modernists as well as others, but as a rule it bulks smaller in their consciousness than it used to do and is no longer the controlling motive of their lives. The modernist, as already noted, is apt to be thinking less of personal salvation than of other things; is apt to find in his religion other values which he counts of greater interest and importance.

For instance religion may have come to mean to him self-realization rather than self-preservation. The latter instinct—a primitive human instinct—underlies the desire for personal salvation, but as the old fears are dissipated with the development of culture, or seem less dreadful than they did, the instinct of self-realization comes into play and finds expression in religion as in many other forms of life. Without question much of the modernism of today is marked by the dominance of this instinct. It is not new. In every age it has made itself felt and in mysticism, both Catholic and Protestant, it has come to expression on a large scale. In this respect mysticism anticipates certain forms of modernism—particularly Roman Catholic modernism—which is more akin in many ways to the mysticism of the Middle Ages than with any other historic phenomenon. Yet there is a striking difference between the older mysticism and the modernist's impulse to self-realization. For the mystic commonly found his higher life apart from the world of men and things while the modernist, at least the Protestant modernist, is not content therewith. He must have a religion which can be realized in and with the world not merely apart from it, which unites a man with it instead of separating him from it, which tends to give oneness to all the parts of

his life instead of separating and dividing them one
from the other. The old dualism which clung to mysticism as well as other forms of Christianity many modernists, Catholic as well as Protestant, have outgrown
completely. The one thing they cannot endure is dualism. Unity, oneness of life is their watchword. The old
instinct of self-realization which found expression in
mysticism functioned in a world which was supposed to
be utterly unlike the world where the self was to come
to full realization, and so there must be opposition and
separation. It is characteristic of the old mysticism that
it was always accompanied by asceticism—a non-ascetic
mystic seemed a contradiction in terms. But the mysticism of the modernist is of a different sort. The present and the future are one. Immediate contact with
God and the ever fuller realization of self in communion with him does not make the modernist less
human, for divine and human are essentially one and
he finds the human most truly and ideally human when
it is most divine.

I have said that it is characteristic of much of the
modernism of today that in it the instinct of self-realization finds larger expression than the instinct of self-
preservation, and that the desire for personal salvation
is therefore less dominant and controlling. But it is
equally characteristic of modernism that the desire for
personal salvation has been crowded into the background by interest in social service and concern for the
welfare of humanity, to which I referred a few moments
ago. Many a modernist has become so absorbed in the

betterment of the world and in the building of the kingdom of mutual love and sympathy and helpfulness within it that he has forgotten all about his own salvation. This is just what Luther wanted and he would have rejoiced with all his heart in the developed social conscience and the splendid social service of modern times. The modernist may not have attained his freedom from fear in the way that Luther did. Much has occurred to make the old evangelical experience unnatural to him. But that is neither here nor there; whether it is because he believes himself already saved as Luther did or for entirely different reasons, at any rate he is now more interested in the welfare of humanity and the building of the kingdom of God among men than he is in his own personal salvation, and religious beliefs and forms and language that are built almost exclusively upon the latter need have become uncongenial to him. Of "finding salvation" or of "getting religion" he has much less to say.

This more than anything else accounts for the fact that so many are entirely outside the churches and make no use whatever of their ministrations, and it accounts also for the fact that within the churches beliefs and practices have changed on a large scale. Probably more than by anything else the modernist is distinguished from the typical Christian of other ages by his relative indifference to personal salvation, as conceived in the past. To escape death, to escape the present evil world, to escape everlasting punishment—multitudes of Christians are less concerned with all this than their fathers were. Immortality no longer intrigues them; the present world they are more interested to improve than to escape from; everlasting punishment they do not believe in.

Often where the old conception of salvation has disappeared and the old language has largely lost its meaning the category of salvation is still retained while its content is more or less completely revolutionized. Many modernists think it important to retain as far as possible the old categories and the old terms, re-interpreting them to correspond with the new ideas. I confess I do not myself approve this practice, not because it savours of duplicity; we are in all spheres of life obliged to re-interpret our terms to meet new situations and we are not guilty of duplicity in doing so. My difficulty is rather that often the retention of the old term, particularly in religion where tradition is so tenacious, prevents the re-interpretation of it from being understood and accepted. It seems to me far better where possible to employ new language to denote new ideas. Of course I know this is not always possible: the history both of philosophy and of science makes this abundantly evident; but when it is possible I think it ought to be done even at the expense of wounding and perhaps alienating sensitive souls who love the old forms of speech.

I have been led to say what I have on this subject by the fact that the term salvation has been retained in the vocabulary of many modernists when the thing itself for which it has traditionally stood and still stands with the great majority of Christians has been lost sight of altogether.

As we have seen, modernists have widely substituted for the old category of salvation—a negative category in which the chief emphasis lay on escape from something undesirable—a different category altogether, namely, enrichment of life or devotion to the kingdom of God. There is of course a negative element in this; enlargement or enrichment of life means escape from the small and the poor life, and devotion to the kingdom of God means escape from lower and narrower devotions. But after all the positive aspect of the matter is here more important than the negative. Indeed one of the important marks of difference between modernism and traditionalism whether Catholic or Protestant is the emphasis it everywhere places on the positive rather than the negative. But where the positive outweighs the negative the term salvation is certainly inappropriate. Throughout Christian history it has appropriately borne a chiefly negative aspect; if we wish to turn attention to the positive we should find another word to take its place and in such words the New Testament itself is not wanting, for after all the word salvation is not so common in the New Testament as is generally supposed.[7]

Closely allied to the change of interest in the matter of salvation is the general abandonment in Protestant circles of the old exclusiveness and intolerance which

[7] To the modernist Christianity is not a religion of personal salvation but of spiritual life; enlargement of personality, of opportunity, of experience— new ideals—new power: to have life and have it more abundantly.   .

found expression in the belief that salvation could be found only in the particular sect of which one happened to be a member. Probably from the beginning there were Protestants who held this more liberal view. At the time of the Reformation three diverse opinions existed. There were those who continued to believe salvation possible only within the Roman Catholic church, and they, of course, remained in that communion. At the other extreme were those who agreed with Luther that salvation was possible only outside the Roman church. They, of course, became Protestants. Probably these two groups made up the mass of the adherents of the Catholic and Protestant churches respectively. But there were also those who thought salvation possible within either the old or the new communion. Of these some went out, others stayed in. Whether there were many such persons it is impossible to say, but there may well have been a large number, particularly of the intellectual class. Erasmus was one of them. He remained in the old church not because he thought salvation impossible outside, but because Catholicism conserved better than Protestantism other values that were precious to him. As time passed and the two wings of the church hardened in their opposition to each other, the two extreme groups tended to grow at the expense of the more liberal group. And this was true as between Protestant sects as well as between Protestant and Catholic. But the liberals never disappeared, and over and over again, at least in Protestantism, they made themselves heard, particularly when sectarianism grew bitter.

This liberalism was the almost inevitable result of the multiplication of sects and the consequent growing conflict of authorities. The conflict of authorities fostered distrust of all authority, and it also tended to make salvation—of which each sect claimed a monopoly—seem less essential. If the outsider could not possibly tell in which of the conflicting sects it was to be found, he was apt to give up seeking it altogether and to conclude it was not worth bothering about. The whole thing hangs together—all these attitudes are but expressions of the common liberal spirit, but in some matters they have been carried much further than in others. Probably for instance multitudes of Protestants conservative enough in other respects recognize the possibility of salvation outside their own sect even though such recognition is itself a sign of liberalism. In this case the liberal attitude has established itself and is now a part of the common Protestant heritage and so may be shared by the most conservative of men.

Another need shared by Catholics and orthodox Protestants is the need of an infallible religious authority. This was found by the Catholics in the church, by the Protestants in the Bible. The infallibility is as complete in the one case as in the other, and the need of it apparently as keenly felt. Here, of course, the Catholics have a great advantage for history proves that the infallibility of a church is a more practical and effective thing than the infallibility of a book. But that is neither here nor there. The point I am making is that while the need of infallibility is common to Catholics and orthodox Protestants it is not ordinarily shared by the modernist.[8] This is not at all surprising. The modern age has been marked by a tremendous growth of human independence and self-reliance, and the tendency has been to subject all authorities to investigation and criticism. Authority is a thing to be tested like anything else, but an infallible authority cannot be tested; it demands absolute and unquestioning submission. The modernist, particularly in a scientific age, is the last man to admit this sort of thing. The whole set of his mind is against it.

There are those who recognize that the claim to infallibility is presumptuous anywhere else than in the sphere of religion, and who find no need of it in other spheres, but in religion they cannot do without it for here man's eternal destiny is involved and there must be infallible assurance about the way of life and everything pertaining thereto. They may believe also that religion is so different in character from other phases of man's life that infallibility may be assumed there when it cannot be anywhere else. But those who have lost the old central interest in personal salvation; to whom religion means primarily something else; those too who have eschewed the category of religious duties and find in right relations with their fellows the real secret of

8 Luther broke with Catholicism because it failed to meet his religious need; modernists with Protestantism for the same reason but also because it bound intellectually.

life and salvation have no more need of infallibility
in religion than anywhere else in life.[9] To them the
distinction set up between religion and the rest of life
in this respect seems artificial and quite unwarranted.[10]

But there is another and historically even more important aspect of the matter and that is the development
of literary and historical criticism. As a consequence of
this development the fallibility both of church and of
Bible has been made abundantly evident. For Protestants historical and literary criticism was not necessary to
convince them that the church is not infallible, that conviction they inherited from the Protestant Reformation,
but such criticism has played havoc also with the alleged
infallibility of the Bible. It is difficult for any man who
recognizes the soundness of the scientific method and is
accustomed to accept the findings of science in other
lines to resist the results of modern Biblical criticism.
He certainly will not do so unless the infallibility of
the Bible is a matter of life and death to him, unless it
seems to him essential to religious faith. Of course if
that be his attitude he may close his eyes to the most
patent facts as multitudes actually do. Or if he must
have an infallible authority whether or no, he may take
refuge in the infallibility of the Bible. But it is evident that where the need of infallibility is not keenly

[9] See McGiffert, "Democracy and Religion," *Religious Education* (June,
1919), pp. 156–161.

[10] For such people the acceptance of truth is no longer the condition of salvation. Salvation is an abandoned category. Formerly infallibility was needed because salvation was so great a thing and was supposed to depend on it. For bodily
health, which was a temporary thing, one could afford to depend on fallible advice. There would be no great harm if the advice were wrong. But health of
the soul was another matter. Here one *must* have the right advice and help.

felt, whether because of the influences I have referred to or for any other reason, the effect of modern Biblical criticism must be to do away with the belief in infallibility altogether.

The change in this matter is a momentous one, leading to the loss of faith in many things which have no vital significance in themselves or no special religious value, but have always been a part of the faith of Christians because recorded in the Bible or contained in the church's creeds.[11]

It is this together with the loss of interest in certain other doctrines of the past because of the fading out of the needs which they met that has led to the notion that modernism is skepticism—that the modernist as distinguished from the orthodox Catholic or Protestant is a skeptic who believes much less than the Fathers believed or has even lost his religious faith altogether. The last accusation is of course a mere calumny. The modernist within the church is as devout a believer as anybody else. He may it is true fail to believe many things the Fathers believed but that is not necessarily because he is instinctively skeptical, though it may be, for agnosticism about things one cannot prove is a fruit of the modern scientific spirit and is shared in greater or less degree by many modernists. But the modernism of our day is in this respect different from the modernism of some other days. It is not skepticism but changing

---

[11] *E.g.*, Virgin Birth, Jonah, the physical resurrection of Christ, and many other miracles.

need that has led to the changing faith. Science offers the modern man as great marvels and mysteries as religion ever did, and whereas a few generations ago much that it teaches would have been dismissed as absurd, it is now willingly accepted even by the most incredulous. The difficulty that the modernist feels with the old system is not that it teaches marvels and mysteries and not that it is too supernatural, but that many of its marvels and mysteries are uninteresting and without significance for the life of today, and that its supernaturalism often impedes instead of enhances religious reverence and devotion. Modern science may teach many things as marvellous as are to be found in any fable or Mother Goose rhyme but they are of a different texture altogether. They are consonant with the whole fabric of scientific knowledge and are not mere meaningless inventions of irresponsible fancy. Similarly the modernist in religion is prepared to recognize phenomena that would have staggered the faith of the Fathers but they must be consonant with the texture of that part of life to which they belong. Religious men must not be asked in the name of religion to accept things on the strength of Biblical or ecclesiastical authority which have no religious meaning and no place in the religious life and experience of today. Life is whole and congruous and must be harmonious with and not contradictory to itself.

GEN. THEO. SEMINARY
LIBRARY
NEW YORK

UNION THEO. SEMINARY
LIBRARY
NEW YORK

Part II

A CONTEMPORARY FAITH

Section A

JESUS

Chapter VI

CHRIST AN ELEMENT IN CHRISTIAN THEOLOGY

The modern age insists on reality. By reality it means that which can be tested either in history or in personal experience. Modern theology, too, must deal with realities. It may draw conclusions transcending experience but these conclusions have worth only as they are inferred from experience and are recognized as inferences. What is true of theology in general is true of Christology in particular.

Christology, or the doctrine of Christ, must be based on the historic Christ. We must begin with him not as the infinite or risen Christ, but as the man Jesus, asking the question, What did he do? The distinction between the Christ of history and the Christ of faith is not sound. Of all Christological theories the doctrine of Kenosis is the most vicious. There is only one Christ.

What, then, has the historic Christ done for the world? What meaning has he for it, or for Christians, or for us? What has he accomplished for us? If he has done nothing we are not Christians. No theology about him may be formulated. He is simply an historic figure without significance. If he has done something so great that we recognize him as our Master and Lord then we are Christians and Christology is our con-

107

cern. It is noticeable that there has always been a theology of Christ, that is, a recognition of his permanent worth for men.

What then has he done? In the first place he has given ethical ideals and purposes. Our moral life is different from what it would otherwise have been had he not lived. In the second place he has given men victory over the world and made them superior to pain and loss and death; a confidence of superiority over all that can hurt or hinder; a freedom from all fear of sin. This we call redemption. He has, furthermore, given men a moral peace and overcome their moral disharmony, which we interpret as divine forgiveness; a moral power, capacity, and incentive, which we interpret as divine sanctification; as well as a confidence in the permanent and independent worth of the human spirit, which we call eternal life. Again, he has given men a new character, new impulses, a new moral spirit. All this we call regeneration.

Christ has also given us a new idea of God. Or we may say he has actually given us God. We believe in God because of Christ. We are sure of him because of Christ. We believe in the Christian God because of Christ; that God is as revealed by Christ and that he has actually established the reign of this God in the lives of men and in our lives.

It is in the light of this which Christ has done that he must be interpreted. What he has done is fact. How we interpret it is theology. The former lies in the ethical and religious sphere and the latter in the sphere of theory. The former is essential; whereas the latter is not. What then of the interpretation?

The interpretation of the work and person of Christ will depend on many things. It will depend on our idea of man; whether he be helpless, depraved and naturally vicious, or whether he be simply blind and in need of light, or strong and needing only incentive. The interpretation will depend on our idea of sin; whether it be a substantial corruption or a depraved will, or on the other hand mere imperfection, a lack of the highest ideals and the like. The interpretation will depend also on our idea of God; whether he be a Christlike God or the avenger of the Old Testament, the holy God, the wrathful God who must be appeased. Finally the interpretation will depend on our philosophy; whether it be in terms of substance or of will, in terms of experiential or value judgments, whether it be monistic or dualistic. The man, it might be said, who has no philosophy has the ordinary substantial realism.

In the past Christ's work has been given various interpretations. His work has been that of a prophet bringing us knowledge of God's will and preaching his kingdom. His work has been thought of as an Incarnation, tranforming the corrupt nature of man by indwelling in him. It has been thought of as Atonement, in the sense of expiation, paying a price to Satan or paying a fine to God or enduring our punishment.

In the past he has been thought to be, first, the Messiah. This is meaningless to us except in the sense of his being the founder of the divine kingdom. His person has been interpreted as the eternal Logos, which is also widely meaningless. Another interpretation of him as the second person of the Trinity, consubstantial with the Father, is also without meaning. In each of these interpretations men have argued back to what Christ must have done from what he was assumed to be. But this is to reverse the order of interpretation which was set forth in the introduction of this chapter.

Under the influence of modern thought two principal ways of interpreting Christ's work have been followed. In line with the monistic philosophy represented by the theology of Schleiermacher, religion is defined as the consciousness of the Absolute. Christ is the supreme manifestation of this consciousness. He is divine as all men are divine, but he is complete and the mediator of the God-consciousness to others or, as Hegel said, the supreme realization of it.

Under the influence of a dualistic, ethical philosophy man is thought of as a spiritual person realizing himself against a malign universe. God, too, is interpreted in terms of purpose. All existence indeed is interpreted in ethical terms. Christ is the one through whom we come to a knowledge of the divine purpose. He has actually brought us to a knowledge of a supreme moral purpose. He has lived that purpose himself and thus mediated it to us by his life as well as by his teaching. He has given us a confidence in its realization, that is to say, he has given us a belief in God, who is interpreted in similar terms. God is God for the fulfillment of Jesus' purpose which we recognize as supreme. And so Christ is divine for us, being the incarnation of the purpose which we recognize as divine.

Whether we shall call Christ divine depends upon what we mean by God. If God is substance then Christ is not divine for there is no evidence of divine substance in him. If God is purpose then this does make Christ divine for there is nothing higher than his purpose. Christ's divinity is a conclusion not a presupposition. Yet it is not immaterial whether we call him divine or not. Such an interpretation has importance as showing our conception of God. It does not hurt Christ not to be called divine. If we recognize his supremacy that is enough. But if we do not call him divine it is because we have another and unchristian idea of God. We seek something in God not found in Christ. We get God elsewhere than from Christ. This procedure is due to the unfortunate fact that our theology is not christianized.

If we ask about the doctrines of Christ's pre-existence, his origin or his resurrection, the answer is that all such questions are unimportant. They are conclusions drawn from our knowledge of what Christ has done. To be sure what he has done may involve the interpretation of his person as having pre-existed. It may involve his supernatural origin. It may involve his continued existence and physical resurrection. Indeed these interpretations most Christians think are absolutely necessary. But even these conclusions, like that respecting his deity, are not directly given facts. The disciples believed in the resurrection because they had seen him. We can believe it only as we have witnessed his activity in us and conclude from that fact his continuing life. Only the given religious fact, however, is essential.

In conclusion it may be stated that the genuine Christian confession is the Lordship of Christ. The one all-sufficient Christian confession is Christ's absolute supremacy. Christ is first. The fault of the Unitarians may be cited to point up this situation. They have begun with God and worked down to Christ. They have failed to make Christ supreme. They have placed another above him. To put Christ in second place in this way is to reverse the historic Christian order. The historic Christian way is just the opposite. It may be narrow but such it is. We recognize as a fact of Christian experience that we have come to God through Christ. We know God through Christ. This our Christian confession is our confession of his deity. The genuine Christian is surer of Christ than of God. The man who believes in Christ and not in God is nearer the historic Christian position than the man who believes in God but not in Christ.

That man makes Christ divine who would stand by Christ whatever experience might say, or whatever other God was offered him. Such a man would stand by Christ, controlling his life by Christ's even if he were convinced that the God of this world were opposed to Christ; or that there were no God. To such a man Christ makes a difference. He recognizes that his own life would have been different if Christ had never lived;

that his ideas and purposes are in some degree dependent on Christ. This man would rather go to defeat with Christ than to victory without him. He would trust him though God himself repudiated him. This is what it means to make Christ supreme and Christ divine.

We believe in God when we believe that Christ will gain the victory, when we believe that the universe is for him and not against him. We believe in God because we trust in Christ. But we trust in Christ anyway, whether there be a God or not. We will follow him and be his. For it is he who has laid hold on us, not God. It is he whom we follow and worship, for he is altogether desirable and to be trusted. Because of him we believe in God. We believe in the rationality, in the goodness, in the divine purpose in the universe because Christ was what he was.

CHAPTER VII

THE LORDSHIP OF JESUS

The Lordship of Jesus finds very frequent expression in our New Testament and other early Christian writings. Thus for instance in Mark 16:19: "After the Lord had spoken unto them, he was received up into heaven and sat on the right hand of God."[1] And in our Apostles' Creed we have all the three particulars referred to in the New Testament, ascension, session at God's right hand, and judgment, associated together in the familiar words "He ascended into heaven, and sitteth on the right hand of God the Father Almighty, from thence he shall come to judge the quick and the dead."

But what do we mean when we use these words today? It is clear that the figures contained in the passages quoted are out of date. For the Copernican astronomy has made it impossible for us to think of heaven as a place above our heads, to which Christ ascended and whence he will come down, and our modern way of looking at things is out of line with the naïve anthropomorphism of the Fathers who pictured Christ as actually seated on a throne at God's right hand. But the antiquated nature of the figures should

---

[1] *Cf.* Acts 7:55; Matt. 26:64; Matt. 16:27; Matt. 25:31.

not blind us to the essential character of the truth expressed by them, a truth which is still valid and still
of significance. Never more significant indeed than today. It is not my purpose to try to set forth all that may
be meant by the Lordship of Jesus, all that may be involved in the belief of the early Christians and of the
church during the ages since when they have called
him Lord. I want to ask simply what elements of this
great truth are of most importance today.

I should say first of all that an essential element in
the Lordship of Jesus is the fact that the purposes of
Jesus are the purposes of God, the ruler of this world.
This is a fundamental Christian truth. "I came not to
do mine own will," Jesus said, "but the will of Him
that sent me." And from the beginning to the end of
his career it was the work of God he believed himself
to be doing and the purposes of God he believed himself to be fulfilling. The truth is wrapped up, indeed, in his recognition of God as his Father, which
underlay all he said and did and suffered. Had his
ideals and purposes been other than the ideals and purposes of God as he understood them, he could not have
thought of himself as God's son and of God as his
Father. And so there should be no question about it.
The Christian God, the God whom Christians worship, whatever may be true of the rest of the world, is
a God who is controlled by the same great purposes
which controlled Jesus, is in fact the same kind of a
God that Jesus was a man. And so if we would know

him we must study, not nature, not history, not our own hearts, but Jesus Christ.

The Christlikeness of God is the one great truth about God for which the Christian revelation stands. "He that hath seen me hath seen the Father," Jesus said, and these words are a significant commentary upon many and various doctrines of God, which have emerged in the history of Christian theology, doctrines taken from a study of nature or of man, from science or philosophy, from human experience or fancy, from the Old Testament or the New, from every other source than from the revelation of Jesus Christ himself. God has been represented by Christian theologians, ancient and modern, as the omnipotent maker and ruler of heaven and earth; as the philosophical absolute, illimitable and indefinable; as at once infinite substance and almighty will; as the great All, in communion with whom we lose our petty individuality and become one with the vast universe of being; as the Holy One, into whose presence no sinner may enter; as the great avenger, who allows no transgression to go unpunished unless it has been duly atoned for; as the supreme sovereign of the universe who for the display of his glorious attributes of justice and mercy chooses some men to everlasting salvation and others to everlasting punishment; as one substance in three persons; as "Spirit, infinite, eternal and unchangeable, in his being, wisdom, power, holiness, justice, goodness and truth." These and many other things Christian theologians have said about God but seldom enough have they said the one Christian thing about him that he is like Jesus Christ, that if we wish to know him, we must study Christ, that only by looking upon the life and character of Jesus can we discover what the Christian God, our God, is. For I would have you notice that it is not simply that Jesus' revelation of God is normative, it is final and complete; not simply that we are to refrain from attributing to God a character out of line with that revealed by Jesus, but that all we know about God we find in Jesus, who was the complete revelation of God to the world and "in whom dwelt the fulness of the Godhead bodily."

The character and purposes of Jesus of Nazareth are, I say, the character and purposes of God. This is the true Christian position and in it is wrapped up the Christian's challenge to the world. If there be a higher God, we may say to the world, show him to us and we will turn from the God and Father of Jesus to worship your God. We will bow before him in adoration and he shall be our God and we his servants. But if there be not, if the Father of Jesus Christ be the highest God we know or can conceive, then let him be your God as he is ours, and let all of us give ourselves as Jesus did to the accomplishment of his purposes and the fulfilling of his will. We could not really remain Christians if we took any other position than this. If we believed that there is a higher God than Jesus' God, that the purposes which actuated him are not the purposes which actuate the supreme God, we could not continue to worship the Christian God and we could not be content to wear the name of Christ, who was leading us to some one other and lower than the true God. And therefore, I say, in asserting that the purposes of God are the purposes which controlled the life of Jesus we are asserting a fundamental truth of our Christian faith, a truth which, if we did not believe, we could not and would not wish to remain Christians. And so if we would know the purpose, above all the supreme purpose of God, we may discover it by looking upon Jesus and learning the supreme purpose which he undertook to accomplish, the purpose to which above all else he devoted his life. For that purpose many have looked elsewhere, to nature, to history, to philosophy, to their own imaginations and ideals. But that purpose, wherever other men may seek it, we as Christians should seek nowhere else than in the life and teachings of Jesus Christ.

And that purpose it is not difficult to discover. Modern critical study of the New Testament has only made it the more evident, so that today the real meaning of Jesus' life stands out with a clearness which it never had in other ages. He came to promote the kingdom of God, a kingdom in which men should give themselves to the doing of the will of God, their Father, in the service of men, their brothers.

Whatever God's relation to the physical universe may be, whatever his cosmical activities, whether he is or is not in all the forces of nature, and whether it is he that speaks in the orderly processes as in the great crises and convulsions of the world is neither here nor there, is in fact of no direct importance to us. A man may believe in the immanence or in the transcendence of

God, he may be a monist or a dualist or a pluralist, all this is immaterial from the Christian point of view and comports equally well with Christianity. The one thing of practical importance for us to know about God is the purpose which he is seeking to accomplish in and through us and other men our fellows, that we may get into line with that purpose and give ourselves to its accomplishment even as Jesus did. To get into line with God's purpose is to be at one with the highest forces in the universe and is to succeed as one can in no other way, is to win a victory over all that would oppose and drag us down, over all the hostile forces of the world, even as Jesus won his victory. For though in all that ordinarily goes to make success, the life of Jesus was a failure, though he suffered poverty, shame, a criminal's death, the world today stamps his seeming failure as a real success, and recognizes his life and his death in the service of the cause for which he stood as the greatest victory history has to show. Others have lived nobly and have died bravely, but it is the life and death of Jesus that have won the world. And that because the purpose for which he lived and died is the highest purpose which we can conceive, to build God's kingdom in this world of ours; not to exploit the world, and to win from it glory, wealth, and power, but to promote the reign of righteousness and love, to set forces in motion which have made not for the mere well-being of himself and of his friends and followers but for the true and permanent betterment of the world. For he came not to save men out of the world, not to establish a church merely but to save the world itself, to make it the kingdom of his God and Father. In the divineness of his purpose we recognize the Lordship of Jesus. He it is indeed that sitteth at the right hand of God, for his purposes are the purposes of God himself.

But again when we assert our faith in the Lordship of Jesus, we declare that his moral standards and principles are the highest known to us, and that we believe they are the moral standards and principles of God himself. What is the greatest of the virtues? One man says truthfulness, another honesty, another justice, another patience, another purity, another humility. Men have given all sorts of answers to the question and Jesus too gave his answer. Not purity, not honesty, not justice, good as these are, but love, the spirit and the purpose of brotherliness. All else Jesus subordinated to this one supreme thing. Not the publican, not even the woman taken in sin was condemned by him, but the righteous Pharisee, who did his complete duty according to the law, but looked upon his fellows with scornful indifference. And not the holy priest or Levite, but the heretical Samaritan, the outsider, was the hero of his greatest parable. This was Jesus' ethical message to the world: "Ye are all brethren," "Thou shalt love thy neighbour as thyself," and "whatsoever ye would that others should do unto you, do ye even so to them." Entering through the knowledge of our own needs and aspirations into an appreciation of the needs and aspirations of our fellows by means of that sympathy which true kinship breeds, we are to spend ourselves and all that God has given us that their needs may be met and their aspirations realized. And when we declare our belief in the Lordship of Jesus we virtually declare our faith that this moral standard of his is the highest standard in the world.

But do we really believe it? Certainly it has not always been believed by Christians. Soon after the days of Christ his followers, over against the corruption of the age, began to emphasize above all else personal holiness, and as time passed the more earnest spirits, finding it difficult to realize their ideal in the midst of the temptations and distractions of the world, went into the wilderness, or into the monastery, there to attain a Christian perfection which they could not among their fellows. The ideal thus expressed finally crowded out completely the ideal of Jesus and the most noble and consistent Christians were believed to be these monks who sacrificed so much for religion's sake, the fact being overlooked that they sacrificed for religion's sake even the principles of Christ himself, whom they professed to follow and to serve. And the same ideal of personal holiness, with a view to personal salvation, has very largely controlled the thinking and the living of the Protestant church as well. For though we have not had our monasteries, we have had our ideal of consistent Christian living as meaning the cultivation of our own spirituality, and with that in view, the avoiding of such-and-such associations, or the eschewing of such-and-such employments. And we have perhaps become

Christians ourselves, or have summoned others to become Christians, in order that we and they may be saved, instead of seeing that the only truly Christian reason for being a Christian is that we may follow Christ in his life of service of his fellows.

And yet though Christians have made this great mistake far too often in the past and perhaps we have sometimes made it ourselves, we realize today clearly enough that it is a mistake. As we look upon Christ we see what the Christian life truly is, and more than that we believe that such a life is the highest life in all the world. If we did not, if, on the contrary, we believed that there is something nobler than following Jesus in his life of self-forgetful service, if we believed that his summons to such a life as he lived is a summons to something lower than the highest, that for men to live with one another in the spirit of true brotherly kindness and helpfulness is not the best way to live, then we certainly should not think of calling ourselves Christians, but we should seek our leader elsewhere, a leader who might show us a loftier and more divine way. By the very fact that we call ourselves Christians, we declare that Jesus' moral standards and ideals are the highest known to us and that they appeal to the very best that is in us.

We may think what we please about the physical power of Christ and about his cosmical activities, we may think of him as working together with God in all the processes of nature, as holding the planets in their orbits and presiding over the succession of the seasons, we may mean all this if we please, when we speak of him as exalted to the right hand of God, but it is entirely immaterial. We may believe it or not, without in any way affecting our Christian faith and life, and it is not for such beliefs as this that we stand today. Whatever may have been the case in other days, today when we assert the Lordship of Jesus, the only thing in the assertion that is of any consequence is that his purposes, his principles, and his ideals are in control, that they represent the highest that the world knows. This we believe and this we stand for, and for this reason we labour to make Jesus' purposes and ideals ever more widely regnant. We believe that society would be morally perfect if his principle of brotherly love controlled absolutely and everywhere all the relations of men with men, and we believe that society would be religiously perfect if his principle of the Fatherhood of God were everywhere realized, so that all men lived with God as children with their father, striving constantly to carry out his purposes and to realize his ideals. We recognize both in Jesus' moral and in his religious principles, ideal principles fitted for the life of man everywhere and always, and so we declare our belief in the Lordship of Jesus, in his exaltation to the right hand of God his Father.

Not simply do we recognize Jesus' principles as of ideal worth and so fitted to control the world, and not simply do we consecrate ourselves as Christians to the promotion of his principles that they may become ever more widely regnant, but we actually recognize that they are more and more dominating the world, and so our creed is not merely a declaration of what we believe ought to be but of what actually is in ever-increasing measure. For as we look into the world about us and then back into the centuries that are gone, we discover that today the thoughts and the lives of men are controlled by the principles of Jesus to a degree true in no other age. Whether the world is growing better or worse is a question often disputed. And whether there is more or less vice and intemperance, lying and stealing, Sabbath breaking and indifference to various religious ordinances, than there once was, may perhaps fairly be debated. But about one thing there can be no possible dispute, the age in which we live is witnessing a more widespread emphasis both within and without Christian circles upon Jesus' great principles of the brotherhood of man, and a more complete realization of it in active helpful service than any age before. This is after all the great test. Recognizing as we do today that in the spirit and purpose of true brotherliness is to be found the highest expression of man's moral nature, we can hardly fail to see that the world is on a higher level than ever before. And unless we shall repudiate our belief in the supremacy of Jesus' ethical principles we cannot doubt that in the end this fuller realization in the world's life of his spirit will bring with it an improved moral tone in all respects. For he who fully enters into Jesus' purpose of service cannot permanently be content with the mere physical betterment of those for whom he labours, he must strive also for their moral uplifting, and for their sakes and not his own alone he must keep himself pure and upright as he tries to make them. And thus in the spirit of Christ which is laying hold so mightily today upon those without as well as those within the church, we may see a power for the moral uplifting of the world more far-reaching and more efficacious than any other ever known. And all this we may give expression to when we declare our belief in the Lordship of Jesus. His is indeed the kingdom, for his principles are taking increasing possession of this world, the world of his Father God.

Finally, the belief in the Lordship of Jesus involves the belief that he is judge, a belief that is expressed in the biblical passages referred to above, as also in the Apostles' Creed, which declares in accordance with New Testament teaching that "He shall come to judge the quick and the dead."

But is not Jesus above all a being of love and mercy, and shall we think of him as judging and condemning any one? Yes, Jesus is love and mercy and so is God his Father. And every man whom God can save he saves, even as Jesus did all he could for every needy person within his reach. But not even Jesus, and not even God his Father can save all. It is not necessary for God to condemn the wicked, the wicked condemn themselves and they pass judgment upon themselves every time they sin, yes, every time they fall short of the best of which they are capable. Let us not be mis-led by the imagery of Scripture. Let us not push the judgment far off into the future, and suppose it means only that at the end of the world the books will be opened and they that have done well will be received into eternal felicity and they that have done ill will be condemned to eternal punishment. The judgment is going on all the time, a judgment passed upon men not by Jesus or by any one else but by themselves, as they fall below their own highest ideals of what they ought to be. And in the future they will not need Christ or any one else to judge them, as they see in the light of the experience of their whole life how far short they have fallen of the man they might have been. What they will need then as now is not a judge but a Saviour, if haply they may be saved. The New Testament means today, and our creed as well, whatever they may have meant in other days of a more crude religious faith, simply that judgment is passed upon men in accordance with the ideals and principles of Jesus. In this sense he is judge as he is Lord. Not are they good or bad, according to the ordinary standards of men the world over, but what are they according to the standard of Jesus, which transcends all others and is the highest that the world has known? Are they living with their fellows in the true spirit of brother-liness, the spirit of Christ? Are they serving to the best of their ability? Are they doing all they can to promote God's good purposes of love for the world? Are they using all their gifts and all their attainments not to promote their own prosperity but to help and bless the world? If not, of what good are they? Were they created for their own sake alone and can they live unto themselves alone? They may, if they will, but in this universe in which we all live, run through and through as it is by the good purposes of God the Father of Jesus, what place is there for one who lives only for himself? And when men come to a full realization of the meaning of it all, how the principle of service is writ large upon it from the highest to the lowest, from God himself to the meanest of his creatures, theirs it will be to pass judgment upon themselves. If they cannot be a part of it, if they cannot come into oneness with God's great and all-controlling purpose, even when they see it in all its beauty and glory, if they cannot even then live with their fellows in the true spirit of brotherhood, and with their God in the true spirit of sonship, they will be glad enough to flee into the outer darkness.

"The kingdom of this world is become the kingdom of our Lord and of his Christ." "Then shall the king say unto them on his right hand, come ye blessed of my Father, inherit the kingdom prepared for you from the foundation of the world. For I was an hungered and ye gave me meat, I was thirsty and ye gave me drink, I was a stranger and ye took me in, naked and ye clothed me, I was sick and ye visited me, I was in prison and ye came unto me. Then shall the righteous answer him saying, Lord when saw we thee an hungered and fed thee, or thirsty and gave thee drink?

When saw we thee a stranger and took thee in? Or naked and clothed thee? Or when saw we thee sick or in prison and came unto thee? And the king shall answer and say unto them, verily I say unto you, inasmuch as ye have done it unto one of the least of these my brethren, ye have done it unto me."

CHAPTER VIII

SAVED BY HIS LIFE

It is a great pity that salvation so early in Christian history was tied up with the death of Christ, for it is not his death that saves us but his life. The reason for attaching salvation to his death instead of to his life is clear enough. His death was the one event that needed explanation. Why, his disciples asked themselves, should such a person as the Messiah die? How was it possible for the Son of God to perish? That he must have died for our salvation seemed a simple and reasonable account of the otherwise inexplicable event.

As to how Christ's death saved men there was no agreement among Christian thinkers until the time of the Middle Ages; but that in some way it did all were agreed. Various explanations of the method were set forth. His death secured salvation by the spilling of blood, by the offering of a sacrifice, by paying a price to Satan, by satisfying the justice of God, or in some other way.

One very serious result of this connection of salvation with Christ's death has been the almost invariable interpretation of salvation in negative terms. Salvation has been interpreted as salvation *from* something—from sin or self or the world or death or punishment—instead of salvation *to* something. This is one of the reasons for the unpopularity of the idea of salvation.

Two things are clear. Salvation that is to be adequate must be positive, not negative. We must be saved to something, to fuller and larger life, to righteousness, for instance, and not just from something. Furthermore, the positive aspect of salvation must precede the negative. No man can be saved from something until he has been saved to something. He cannot first be saved from sin and then afterwards be introduced to righteousness. He cannot first be saved from self and then afterwards be given some object to live for. Nor can he first be saved from death and then afterwards be given life. Christian leaders would do well to remember this in all their work. Give men something good, something high and fine, to live for; as they live for it they will turn from their sin.

How are we to think of Christ's life as saving men? To put it briefly, Christ saves us by his life in two ways: first, by showing us the ideal life, the new life to which we are saved if we are saved at all; and secondly, by giving us power to live that life, the power that comes from the pressure upon us of his ideal and his example and still more from fellowship with him. The pressure of his personality upon ours is our source of power.

It is widely the fashion among modern men to deny the notion of salvation. This is a great mistake, though such men are right in repudiating a negative salvation. Salvation was never more needed than now. But it is important that the old Catholic and Evangelical idea of salvation be transformed, and that it be interpreted in positive terms.

Christ's saving work did not begin nor did it cease with Calvary or Easter. The salvation he brings is the salvation that consists in serving a great cause, the salvation of a richer and more abundant life. And our fellowship with him is a fellowship with the living Christ, not the dead Christ. We are saved by his life.

CHAPTER IX

THE LIVING CHRIST

I have sometimes felt that Easter Day, on which the attention is apt to be centred wholly in the marvellous occurrence recorded in the closing chapters of the gospels, frequently contributes to doubt rather than belief; that the uniqueness of the event and the sort of testimony we have for it breed skepticism rather than faith. At any rate unless the event is connected in some way with the age in which we live, unless it still has vital significance for our modern life, I hardly see how we can go on accepting it indefinitely. But it is my own conviction that it is vitally connected with our age—that it really means a living Christ still active and powerful among us. If it did not mean this, I confess it would have little interest to me—a curious fact, if it was a fact, but nothing more.

"Why seek ye the living among the dead?" Let us reflect a little upon the contemporary aspect of Jesus' resurrection.

Where it is believed that Christ still lives and works among us, of course the particular form the resurrection took and the particular incidents of the resurrection morning seem unimportant. The big fact is that Christ still lives and that he is to be found not among the dead but among the living. This makes the resurrection of vital and continuing worth.

If Christ, after rising from the tomb, at once disappeared again, and has never been seen since, his resurrection concerns us little. The old Deistic idea of God as a being who created the world and then took his hands off and left it to run without any interference from him led almost inevitably to atheism. If God is not present and active, he might as well be dispensed with altogether. But religious men could not put up with such a conclusion, and hence they could not long rest content with a deity who, like the gods of Epicurus, was for all practical purposes the same as no god at all. As a result there grew up the belief in divine immanence, and God was brought back again into the very heart of the world—a living and present reality. Thus the atheism which had seemed the necessary consequence of natural science and of the critical philosophy was overcome.

Similarly with the resurrection of Christ. If it be simply an isolated event, occurring in Palestine nineteen hundred years ago, it will surely cease ultimately to be a part of the belief of the modern man and Christians will learn to get on without it altogether. If on the other hand it links itself up with a living Christ, part and parcel of the life of today—it will continue to engage the faith of Christendom.

But what do we mean by a living Christ, a Christ still with us and among us? Paul believed in the living

Christ; but many things have happened since his day and it is not easy for the modern man to think exactly as he thought. His dualistic philosophy of substance, taken over from the contemporary Hellenistic world, is not congenial today. To be sure he ethicized the whole matter in a remarkable degree, but the substantial and physical categories still remained and it was these the Catholic church seized upon and translated into mystical and magical formulæ in its doctrine of the sacraments. There are many who still think in sacramental terms, but most of us cannot and do not care to. We praise the Christian life ethically rather than physically, and if Christ be still alive and present with us he must show himself in ethical rather than in physical ways—not by visions, or voices, or spirit-writing, or table-rapping, or similar spiritistic phenomena, but in moral ideals and incentives, in moral influence and achievement.

It is just this we certainly discover as we study the history of modern Christendom. We are witnessing a tremendous growth in Christian ideals. They are not static things enunciated by Jesus himself and continuing unchanged ever since. They are dynamic; full of life, and developing all the time to meet our modern conditions; creating new forms and expression for themselves almost with every generation that passes.

The Christian conscience of today is sensitive on many matters on which the conscience of our fathers was obtuse, though they were just as good and just as well-intentioned as we. Slavery, the drink and drug traffic, religious liberty, the emancipation of women, the equality of all before the law, the economic status of the working classes, the relations of capital and labour, social service, internationalism, and the like—all these we are awake to as they were not.

The fulfillment of our ideals may leave much to be desired—perhaps as much as ever it did—but it is quite certain that our ideals are rising and rising rapidly. Moreover it is equally certain that these ideals, which are emerging generation by generation, are Christian ideals. Not that they are necessarily to be found in the teaching of Christ—he never criticized slavery or religious persecution or child labour, and he never had anything to say about international relations. And yet we are well aware that his spirit is speaking in them and that at any rate the best of them are genuinely Christian ideals, even though they may have come from many sources. Wherever they started they have been baptized in the name of Christ and are as truly a part of our existing Christian morality as any of the principles and precepts that have come down from an ancient past.

All this means that Christ's spirit is not dead but alive; not static but dynamic; not bound and stereotyped, but free and creative. Is Christ still alive and present among us? What more could he do if he really were? Is not his spirit moving forward with us in this great advance of the human spirit? Is he not leading us and beckoning us to follow as he did in the days of his earthly career?

We often hear the cry in these modern days: "Back to Christ." The last thing we want to do is to go back to Christ or to anybody else. Rather we should say: "Forward with Christ," forward into ever new adventures of the spirit, into ever better ways of living, into ever larger moral achievements. Of course, this does not mean forward with a new and unknown Christ, the creation of our own imagination, the child of the age in which we live. Doubtless there are those to whom it means just this, but they who have faithfully and persistently studied the Jesus of the Gospels, they who have saturated themselves with his teachings and have absorbed his spirit, as they have followed him in his ministry, listening to his revealing words, and watching his gracious deeds, they know him and cannot be deceived by false Christs. Only the man thus equipped to recognize the real Christ can be a safe leader of the church in these modern days.

I have said that the living Christ is to be found in the advancing ethical ideals of the modern world. The living Christ is to be found also in our Christian faith in the future, in our faith in a better world yet to be —a faith often derided and yet the real secret of all the moral advance we are making. What does this faith mean if not a living instead of a dead Christ? Not thus do the dead function. The spirit of Christ must be very much alive to create even in the midst of the most disheartening disillusionments this abiding faith in better things to come, a faith in which are rooted the labour and the sacrifice that will alone make those better things actual. It is not a dead Christ we have to do with, but a Christ full of life—ideals that are creative, that are growing and developing all the time, and a faith that is never satisfied but is reaching forth always to a better and a nobler future.

When Christ died on Calvary his spirit certainly did not leave the earth. After nineteen hundred years it is still alive and active among us, never more alive indeed and never more active and creative than today. We may have difficulties about the bodily resurrection. We may think it a crass and primitive way of giving expression to a spiritual reality, but of the spiritual reality itself we may be very sure. The death of Jesus did not mean the passing of the spirit that was his, for that spirit is still with us and in it is our great hope for the coming of the kingdom of God.

But it is not simply a question of ideals and of faith; there is also moral power here that testifies to living force and not mere dead futility. However it is to be accounted for it is certain that multitudes of people find in Christ inspiration and strength for daily living. It may perhaps be explained, if you will, simply as the influence of his words and his example as recorded in the Gospels. But what more could there be if he were actually alive among us? Could the inspiration be any greater than it is, and the pressure of spirit on spirit any more compelling? Are there not many in our own day as devoted as Jesus' immediate disciples were? A person who can still arouse the loyalty and devotion of countless men and women, who can incite them to better living, to self-sacrificing service, is for them at least no dead figure. Not thus do we follow the dead. Only as for us they are alive can they dominate our lives as Christ still dominates the lives of his disciples.

Let me urge you to seek the living among the living, not among the dead; to look for Christ not in the empty tomb in Palestine, but in the idealism and faith and devoted effort of this our own day and generation; to see him in the van of moral progress just where the adventure is greatest and the creative spirit most alive.

It is no dead Christ we dedicate ourselves to; no mere figure of an ancient past; no unchanging code written on tables of stone; no lifeless conventionalities suited only to a bygone age; no provincial ethics good only for the simple society of Palestine in the first century of our era. It is a living Christ and a growing and developing Christianity we believe in.

Those who are eager to keep Christianity close bound with the fetters of the past, who think it was complete in the first century and should never be allowed to grow or change, seem to me to have missed altogether the real significance of Easter Day, the real meaning of the resurrection of Christ. At the very heart of Christianity is life, and life means inevitably growth and change. If in these modern days we can still preach Christianity to a modern world, it is just because it is a living, growing thing; because its leader is alive, not dead, and is in advance of our modern world, not lagging behind it in the mists of the first century.

"Why seek ye the living among the dead? He is not here, he is risen." *There* is the charter of our Christian liberties; *there* is the warrant of our Christian progress; *there* is the ground of our assured faith in a better Christianity and through it in a better world yet to be.

But I am not sure we have got to the heart of the matter yet. Suppose the living Christ really were with us, what would be our experience? Would not our hearts burn within us, even if we did not recognize him? Could he be walking at our side, and we not feel the joy of his presence, even if our eyes were holden, as were those of the disciples on the road to Emmaus? And is not this experience of joy and inspiration exactly the experience of the man who is doing Christ's work, following in his footsteps, living in his spirit? Is there not something about it that transcends the common life? Men have thought they had visions of Christ in their monastic cells, but no vision of theirs can equal that of the man who is really doing Christ's work, serving as he served, and living in his spirit day by day.

It may be he thinks he has no vision. It may seem to him he sees nothing others do not see, for if he is really walking with Christ he is clothed in humility. But when he has once known the glow of Christian service—whether he calls it Christian service or not—let him abandon it and put his life to other and selfish uses and see if he has not descended from the mount of vision to walk in unillumined ways.

Fellowship with the living Christ! If there be a living Christ those that do his will certainly must walk in that fellowship even though they realize it not.

But you say, Is not this the same as fellowship with God? And I reply, Of course it is. Paul was right when he spoke of God in Christ. Unless we find God in Christ, it is of course vain to talk about the living Christ at all. It is not as a mere human figure that Christ is with us. We are not talking about spiritism. It is the divine Christ that is here. If we find God in the historic Christ, if looking upon him we see God ("He that hath seen me hath seen the Father")—if looking upon him we see the purpose of God and the redeeming grace of God incarnate, then we find God also in the living Christ.

I for one cannot distinguish in my own experience between the living God and the living Christ. The doctrine of the Trinity so far as it means a distinction between Son and Father is in my opinion not a doctrine of experience at all but of philosophy. But it is the experience of Christians that, as they find God in the Jesus of the Gospels, so now they find him in the living Christ, working out his divine purposes, illuminating the minds of his children, imparting to them of his power, kindling their joy, offering himself for fellowship with them as they respond by giving themselves eagerly and gladly to the doing of his will, to the sharing of his holy and gracious purposes.

"Why seek ye the living among the dead? He is not here, but is risen."

And is there resurrection for us too? The question is inevitable. Cut off in youth when our work is but just begun, or cut off in advanced years when a long life-time of labour and service lies behind us, is it all at an end when death strikes us down? Of course it is not at an end if the influence of what we have done lives on after us. Any of us might well count that enough and thank God for it. But is that the whole tale? I take it there is a living Christ today because there was a man Jesus in whom the divine purpose incarnated itself, and so long as the divine purpose lives he must live. I take it too that *wherever* there is a human life in which the divine purpose incarnates itself there is eternity, there is real victory over death and time.

CHAPTER X

THE UNSEARCHABLE RICHES OF CHRIST

Poverty is the trouble with our Christianity and with our preaching. We do not realize the wealth that resides in Christianity. We read the gospel too narrowly and make it too easy. We see that we must study the world, labour conditions, and so on, and we overlook the need of studying the gospel. What in fact are we doing to learn about the unsearchable riches of Christ? Yet this is our great duty. The gospel is our gift to the world. If we do not give it to the world, the world will not get it, and the world will organize itself without us.

Evangelicalism is at fault. Its gospel is too simple. The modern social emphasis is quite as much at fault with its equally simple gospel. But neither of these is the whole Christ. Each represents one phase only, and there are fathomless riches besides. Christianity has been in the world 1900 years, and yet how little we have learned of Christ! How shallow our knowledge of him! What the world needs is more of Christ; not simply more of his gospel. That is only a part. Of course it is needed, but it is not enough. We need more of Christ himself—his convictions, his ideals, his character, his atmosphere. We need greater familiarity with him in all his aspects and attitudes; in his life among his people; his purity—a purity that pities and associates with impurity; his love—that unites all men and binds together even the most unlike, and embraces all; his piety—that leads him to reverence God and all men. If we read Christ's gospel in the light of the whole man, it would mean much more to us.

Christ is the world's greatest possession, and the world should know more of it and get more of its value out of it. Christ is not a mere example to whom we can refer the question: "What would Jesus do?" He is a spiritual power in which we can dip and find strength, with whom we can commune, on whom we can draw. There is no distinction between the historical Jesus and the living Christ. The latter is simply the former realized, entered into, enjoyed, used.

Yet we cannot make Christ known to the world unless we know him; nor his wealth known unless we know him richly. He is big enough for all time and the minister's greatest business is to make Christ known, the whole Christ; not a doctrine about him but himself, not his mere words but the man that spoke through the words. Formerly we had an elaborate theology and in revolt we have tried to simplify it. But the trouble was not that the theology was elaborate, but that it was unreal. It was not Christ we were giving men, but philosophy, metaphysics, speculation, and the like.

The historic Christian faith is that Christ is the manifestation of God, that in him dwelt the fullness of the Godhead bodily. Hence to know him is to know God. He is as exhaustless and as permanent as God.

No age can go beyond him. If it thinks it can that is because it does not know him. The great difficulty always is that we read Christ too narrowly and make him too small. The Unitarians are not alone guilty of this. Often the Trinitarians have been equally guilty, and Unitarianism is sometimes a protest not against making too much of Christ, but too little. This failure to apprehend the whole Christ revenges itself, for when the particular age is past, Christ seems passé, too, since the partial aspect previously stressed is no longer important. It had seemed all there was, and so we say he is outworn. We must show the world that Christ is not outworn and never will be, that an exhaustless being like him will meet all the needs of all men of all ages.

CHAPTER XI

WHAT MAKES A CHRISTIAN?

The notion of what makes a Christian has changed. Formerly the important thing was the holding of various beliefs, such as the Nicene or Apostles' Creed, or membership in a church. Now in accordance with the saying "Not every one that saith, but he that doeth" it is Christian discipleship that makes a Christian. The amount of belief has been reduced, but activity has taken its place. So a Christian *may* be without belief in God, or Christ may be his God, or he may believe in one or another kind of God. His God may not be Christian at all. It may be Jewish, as Jesus' God was. It may be neo-Platonic. It may be Stoic or Hindu. It may be Deistic. Christianity is a great world religion and may include all temperaments and all possible attitudes toward God. God serves many needs, physical, intellectual, moral, social. Therefore we should always encourage any communion with God that one may find it possible to enjoy, but we must not lose sight of the Christian God and his purpose for the kingdom. We must insist that faith in God is an achievement. No one can inherit it, or get it except by effort. God is not a mere explanation of the universe. One may be a Christian and have a very unchristian or non-Christian idea of God, as one may have unchristian ideas of many things, the Bible, the world, man, and the like. But there is a Christian idea which is due to Christianity and is the fruit of it.

To be a Christian is to follow Christ in labour for the kingdom. To have a Christian God is to have a God whose will this is. God is not first, but Christianity is first. One may start with a God, with any God, but the Christian God is to be had only from Christianity. The God of a Christian does not mean the God any Christian may happen to have, any more than the "mother of a Christian" or the "dress of a Christian," but the God that matches Christianity, the God that is correlative to the Christian principle or the fruit of it. It means the God that is fitted to Christianity rather than to something else, a fruit of Christianity, like all other theology.

We do not begin with the Christian God, but we begin with Christ. He is the way to God. No way to God is needed if one has God already. The Christian God may not be taken for granted in Christianity, but is led up to. Christ is his messenger and his revealer. What do we find out from Christ about God? He is a God of love. What does this mean? Not that he is concerned with our happiness or well-being, but with the promotion of love among men. God is an active spirit, not a mere passive emptiness or substance. He is a personal being. No other God is worth while. One may say that God as infinite substance is easy to believe in, but not God as purpose or person. Well, that means simply that one has not risen to the level of the Christian God. "There are gods many and lords many."

What is the process? It is following Christ, recognizing his purpose, finding it divine, and then getting faith and confidence and cheer and backing from this faith. We may begin with God as love, as a child recognizes his mother's love very early. But it may be long before the child finds anything more in his mother. There may be nothing more there, her love mere empty love, or unintelligent, purposeless love. To many God is no more than this. But certainly this is not the Christian God. This is only an idol, as Fichte said. It is not enough to say "God is love." We must analyze this and see what it means.

A Christian is a man who has the same need of God as any other man and gets from him much the same as any other man. But I am speaking here of the Christian God, as distinguished from the God of others. This God is identical with the Jewish God in his general purpose, to found the kingdom among men.

We cannot ask what Christianity is to be in all times to come, but what it is to me, now; and God must correspond. If we have a God, then Christianity must be his will, and when we know what Christianity is, we know what God is. We must start with the *nearer*, not the farther. We must not learn what Christianity is from what God is, but vice versa. We must start with Christ. According to George William Knox, "Service of our fellows introduces us to the Christian God." We cannot know forgiveness or love until we forgive and love. They are an achievement, a hard thing, not an easy thing. Temple and ritual stimulate feelings of awe and mystery in the presence of the infinite God. So mercy and love and service stimulate gratitude and love toward the God of self-sacrificing devotion, who gave his Son, which involved as great or greater suffering for him as for Christ. To be a Christian has often meant to be a Buddhist under another name (asceticism), or a Mohammedan (fighting for God), or a Jew (worshipping God and keeping his law); but for us to be a Christian is to promote the kingdom of God, and God must be this. This is what the love of God means for us.

Belief in God to the Christian is a means, not an end. For the modern Christian God exists for the sake of the ideals which are precious to the Christian. If these ideals are realizable it is because they are rational, because they are in line with and not opposed to the universe in which they must be realized, because divinity is at the heart of things and the ideals themselves are divine. This is the faith brought by the Christian message, and this faith the life of Jesus guarantees. The pragmatic venture of faith is confirmed in the life of Jesus. The world recognizes Jesus' victory. This means that the world recognizes the validity as well as the beauty of his ideas, that is, their divineness. Religious faith is the support of our ideals. The ideal once recognized as God's commends itself to many who did not before accept it and to others who did. The fact that it is God's gives new enthusiasm and courage to the Christian.

Section B

GOD

Chapter XII

GOD AND HUMAN NEED

Men believe in God because they need him. If the time should ever come when they were sufficient unto themselves; when all their needs were adequately met without God, they would forget that there was a God and the faith of the fathers would be buried in oblivion. The daily events of life, the physical realities all about us which we see and touch, we believe in because we cannot help it. We are forced to accept them and make the best of them whether or no. But "No man hath seen God at any time." And any man if he will may refuse to credit the fact of God's existence and go his way without him.

Even by those who believe in God the need of him is not always felt with a like vividness. At times we seem to get on very well without the thought of him. At times again we are recalled to our need of him in peremptory fashion. Failure in business; the miscarriage of some project we have set our hearts upon; disaster to a cause or an institution to which we have given our best efforts; the entrance of death into the family circle, taking from us, with some loved form, all the joy and hope of life; a sudden calamity plunging a whole community into mourning and reminding every one of the fleeting character of human life and the precarious nature of human plans—by such events as these we are often driven back upon God and our eyes are opened to the need of him, to the need of his eternity to put meaning into these brief lives of ours and into the work which we devote ourselves to for a few short years and then lay down for good.

It is of this aspect of human need that I would speak; the need of faith in God to give our lives meaning and our work true worth. We may enrich our lives and enlarge their significance by bringing them into vital and helpful connection with the lives of those about us. As we come to recognize that we are not isolated individuals, living unto ourselves alone, but are a part of the great human family, sharing its destinies, endowed with its privileges, and weighted with its burdens, our vision broadens and life takes on a new meaning for us. As we grow older and the ambitions of youth fail to realize themselves and the infinite possibilities of life, which kindled our enthusiasm as we stood upon its threshold, dwindle to pitifully small proportions, it is a great inspiration to find a work transcending the limitations of our own narrow existence and circumscribed calling. Social service, civic reform, municipal improvement—all these have furnished new interests to multitudes of lives which threatened to grow stale and unprofitable. In this felt need of broadening life and giving it greater worth lies without doubt the secret not only of the growing multiplication of occupations both for men and women, and the increasing entrance of the latter into commercial, professional and public life, but also of much of our modern humanitarianism. Not all of it to be sure, for the natural instincts of sympathy and helpfulness and the consecrations of religion have also had their part in promoting it. But that social service is carried on today on a much larger scale than ever before is due not to the fact that we are different from the fathers and better than they but, in part at least, to the terrible contrast in this modern age between the powers of man and the seeming vanity of human life. Never before was the race so conscious of its strength as now. Never before was it in possession of so vast a range of knowledge, or in control of so many of the forces of nature. No wonder the age is marked to an unprecedented degree by human self-confidence and self-reliance—by the spirit of work and the lust of achievement. And yet in spite of it all men are but mortal. Modern medicine and surgery have made tremendous advances, but death at best is only postponed a little. Its inevitableness is in no degree lessened.

In the sharpness of this contrast between human ability and human mortality—a contrast never so acute as today—lies the crying need of the age for occupations and activities whose significance and worth shall not be measured by the brief span of a man's life. It is just here I am inclined to think we find our greatest need of God today.

Faith in God has met many and various needs. There is the physical need of protection against all sorts of ills—earthquake, famine and pestilence; perils of land

and sea; enemies of earth and air; suffering, sickness and death. In earlier ages particularly it was such needs as these that led most men to believe in God. Intellectual needs also have suggested faith in God: to explain the beginning of things; to account for the origin and preservation of all that is; to solve the riddle of existence, the whence and whither of human life; to put unity back of multiplicity and reality back of ever changing appearance.

Moral needs too have given rise to faith in God: the need of a moral lawgiver, moral sanctions, moral standards and ideals, moral strength and betterment, forgiveness and inward peace of conscience. All of these make their influence widely felt in our own day as in earlier days, but none of them can be called the peculiar and characteristic need of this age. That lies rather in the desire to discern worth and significance in human life that we may thus justify the possession of powers and capacities seemingly so disproportioned to the use we can make of them here.

Belief in God meets this need as perhaps nothing else can by giving permanent meaning to these lives of ours and to the work we are doing in this earth.

In two ways belief in God may do this:

1. In the first place by giving us the assurance of human immortality and thus endowing our lives directly with the gift of permanence. If there be a God we may well entertain the hope of a life beyond the present, but if there be not the hope can hardly be other than a vain dream. The influence of the doctrine of

immortality is, of course, to magnify and dignify the human soul. Heir of eternity, it cannot be thought meanly of nor the life it lives regarded as of small account. Probably no other belief has counted for so much in promoting the sense of human worth. No man can think contemptuously of himself or of another who is vividly alive to the fact of the soul's everlasting destiny. Sometimes doubtless the conviction has affected life unhappily, by substituting interest in another world for interest in this world, or by reconciling people to social and economic conditions here which ought not to be tolerated. It has often been all too easy to stop the complaints of the oppressed and to quiet the conscience of the oppressors by the thought of a future life when all will be well. But this, of course, is an abuse of a belief which should have the effect of making human life too valuable ever to be trifled with and too sacred ever to be profaned.

In these modern days of enlarged human abilities it would seem as if the desire for immortality must be more widely and keenly felt than ever before, as if the contrast between the consciousness of human power and the brief opportunity for its exercise here on earth must greatly increase the longing for a future life. But strangely enough this can hardly be said to be the case. It is true that modern psychical research has promoted interest in it here and there and more is being written upon the subject than a generation ago. It is true also that the war with its terrible wastage of young and vigorous life kindled the hope of immortality and the belief in it in many quarters where both had largely faded out. And yet there are probably more persons both within and without the Christian church who are indifferent on the subject than in any other period of Christian history.[1]

This indifference is a new thing in Christian history. Not many generations ago the doctrine of immortality was a fundamental tenet not only of orthodox Christians but also of Unitarians, rationalists and even Deists. They all alike regarded it as essential to morality as well as to religion. Today this is far from being the case. It is not that this life has become so superlatively good that men do not care for another. This might easily—as it often does—promote the desire for the indefinite continuance of life elsewhere if not here. Nor, on the other hand, that it has become so miserable that men long to get rid of it altogether and slip back into the peace of nothingness. This spirit has always existed. Certainly there is no more of it now than in other days if as much. Nor is it because of the growth and dominance of materialism. There is less materialism now than often in the past and it is a fact today that many of the most thoroughgoing idealists are equally indifferent touching another life in another sphere.

It is rather, for one thing, that interest in the present world and in its future has been greatly enhanced by the development of modern science and the multiplication of modern inventions and discoveries. This world of ours is far more fascinating and in spite of the disil-

---

[1] The title of Lowes Dickinson's Ingersoll Lectures of a few years ago, *Is Immortality Desirable?* will occur to many in this connection. The significant fact is not the prevalence of disbelief in immortality but the widespread lack of interest in it on the part of so many people, Christians included.

lusionments of the war it is far more promising than it once was. To this may be added the influence of the modern scientific tendency—felt by common people as well as by scientists themselves—to accept and to regard as important only what can be verified in experience.

But these considerations do not wholly explain the situation. As a matter of fact what the man of today particularly longs for is not another existence elsewhere but larger opportunities here. His life may be dignified and given permanent worth by the gift of immortality but this is not enough. Not alone the man himself but his work must be glorified. It is not a heaven of repose or of contemplation he desires but of activity, of tasks of abiding significance and adequate to his powers. The best guarantee of human immortality is the immortality of the cause for which men work; the best ground of hope in it the large service they are fitted to perform when life ends and earthly activity ceases. Not necessarily that personality cannot die but that personality engaged in the doing of a great work and enlisted in the promotion of a great cause may well count for too much in the divine economy to be allowed to perish.

If we would promote and make more vigorous the belief in immortality among our fellows, we must show that it means the permanence of man's task and not simply of his person. Not length of life alone but quality of life is the essential thing. The cause to which men devote themselves now and here must be worthy of their powers if their earthly careers are to seem other than a mockery. The cause must be immortal whether they themselves are or not. Only if it be immortal is immortality worth while.

2. The second way in which faith in God meets the need of the modern world is by putting this quality of permanence into the object for which men labour. When we reach the conviction that a divine purpose permeates this universe, and that God is at work in the world accomplishing his holy will and building the kingdom of righteousness and peace and love and sympathy among his creatures, and that to give oneself to the promotion of this kingdom is to be labouring with him for an eternal end, then life here as well as hereafter takes on a richness of meaning otherwise undreamed of. Every effort made and every achievement won by us counts permanently in God's great plan. Nothing we do is wasted. We may remain here only a little while, but our life has an eternal worth because it has been used for eternal ends.

We may emphasize other aspects of Deity if we choose—his absoluteness, his omnipresence, his infinity, his self-existence—but the Christian God is above all else he whose holy and eternal purpose for the world the prophets proclaimed and Jesus of Nazareth lived before the eyes of men.

Not least among the benefits of faith in such a God is the broad vision it gives to those who share it. Enlargement of view is in it and the wisdom that comes therefrom. Men may be unselfish and devoted in their work but if their horizon is narrow and their outlook limited, if they think only of the immediate effect

and measure success by present results, their work
will mean much less than it might. To acquire a sense
of divine purpose is to possess a controlling and cor-
rective principle of tremendous value. The habit of
looking at things in the large, of connecting them with
the past and the future, of estimating their tendencies
—this is the habit of wisdom.

And belief in God gives men not simply a sense of
the past and the future, but also oneness of sympathy
with all other workers. If a divine purpose underlies
this world it may be apprehended by them as well as
by us. The ideal is not our private property discovered
by ourselves or our fathers alone. Its witnesses must
be everywhere, and through all men of good will it
must be working itself out in one and another way. To
realize our oneness with others in the promotion of a
common task, this is a prime requisite to the success of
the work. Not in isolation, not in proud self-sufficiency,
but in co-operation lies the secret of success. If the divine ideal seems long in realizing itself in this world
of ours, it is due to our slowness not alone in opening
our eyes to God but in opening our hearts to our fellows.

It is here the Christian church has its place. Truly
understood it is nothing more nor less than organized
co-operation for the accomplishment of God's holy will
in this world, and it ought to be as wide as conscious
human effort to that great end. No difference of form
and ceremony, of doctrine and government, should keep
those apart who are labouring in the common cause. No

narrowness of outlook and meanness of sympathy should interfere with their fellowship in faith and service. The church is a standing witness as it has always been to human belief in the everlasting God, and in this lies its marvellous fascination and the secret of men's loyalty to it. Serving the church they have felt sure that their work had permanent worth and their brief lives eternal meaning. And if we in these modern days would command like loyalty to the service of humanity we must invest it with like worth and meaning by linking it to the eternal purpose of God.

With wisdom and sympathy comes also from our faith in God a steadiness and resoluteness of purpose to be gained in no other way. Things may often seem to be going badly. Discouragement is bound to dog the footsteps of him who depends for confidence upon daily evidences of the success and value of his work. But if he has committed himself to a cause he believes to be God's cause, he gathers constant support from his faith and is able to move calmly through bright days and dark days, through good report and ill.

Inspiration, courage, joy, wisdom, steadfastness, and world-wide and age-long co-operation in the promotion of ends of universal and eternal worth—all this faith in God may mean to a man. But may not such faith have its dangers? Has not the thought of eternity often made the present seem so small as to be hardly worth considering? Has not the conviction that the work is God's work relieved men of responsibility, and the confidence that he will certainly accomplish his own good ends given them an easy and indolent optimism which has sapped the nerve of human endeavour?

Doubtless this has often been the case but the fault has lain, not in the recognition of divine purpose but in the misinterpretation of it. If a man's faith in God be the fruit of selfishness, or indolence, or incapacity, then the recognition of divine activity may serve as a sedative rather than an inspiration. God's work may be a substitute for ours instead of its support. But if belief in God be the answer to our need of discovering worth and meaning in our life and work it cannot relieve us of our task without stultifying itself. We seek, indeed, not a God to do our work but to make our work worth doing. And the God we find is not one who works without us and independently of us, building his kingdom in the world despite the indifference and hostility of men. He is a God who works through men and through them alone. The doing of the work is not God's but man's. Only as men labour for the kingdom will it ever prevail in this world. God's place it is to illumine and inspire the minds and hearts of his children that they may make his end theirs and carry it to accomplishment under his guidance and in the power of his Spirit.

Our faith in the ultimate victory of the divine purpose rests not upon our belief in God's interference in the affairs of the world, or in a miraculous cataclysm overturning the existing conditions and relationships of life, but upon our confidence in the power of the divine character so to impress and influence the motives and the conduct of men that by their own labour and toiling they will bring in the kingdom of God. Our faith rests upon the conviction that the Christian gospel in which the mind of the God we worship comes to clearest expression is of so compelling a nature that it must master the minds and hearts of men when they shall once apprehend it in all its beauty and glory. Not by destroying human freedom or denying human agency, but by evoking human loyalty, devotion and enthusiasm does God accomplish his good will in this our world. Upon us depends the outcome, but we know it is secure, for he who has laid hold upon us and mastered our hearts and lives will lay hold upon countless others, mastering their lives and hearts in ever more compelling fashion as the generations pass and humanity's witness to the goodness and power of God gathers ever greater cogency.

How then may we reach this faith in God if we have it not—or how may we confirm it if it has found lodgment in our hearts? There is but one way—"He that doeth my will shall know of the doctrine," Jesus said. It is the true method of faith. You may study history in vain. You may examine the evidence of goodness in the world and find it so offset by evil and wickedness that you fall into a very slough of despond. But make the venture of faith; give yourself to a high and noble task; and labour and keep on labouring in spite of everything for the promotion of the reign of righteousness and peace, of love and mercy, of sympathy and service among men, and it will dawn upon you with increasing clearness that you are in league with God, that, in spite of the frustrations of war and the heartbreaking disappointments of peace, the highest forces in the universe are actually working with you, not against you.

If you know not whether the world be God's world, determine that you will do your part to make it Godlike and lo! in the end, if not yet, you will find God in it. Such faith comes not to the indifferent and indolent, to him who merely looks on. It is a faith to be won, not to be received as a gift. It belongs in highest measure only to heroic souls who dare to venture everything.

Chapter XIII

CHRISTIAN THEISM

The gods of Christendom have been many and various. Christians are men and they have the instincts and needs of our common humanity. As other men do they generally need a god to worship and adore, a god whom they can look to for protection, for strength, for prosperity, for comfort and for happiness in this life and the next; a god to obey and to give them laws and moral standards and sanctions; a god on whom they can depend, in whom they can trust, to whom they can trace the origin of the world, and by whom they can explain all things including their own lives and the lives of their fellows. These varied needs they often find met by a god who is no whit different from the gods of other religions, who is Christian, if Christian at all, only in name.

Moreover the theistic ideas that have prevailed within the Christian church have come in large part from pre-Christian and extra-Christian sources. The disciples started with the God of the Jews whom Jesus worshipped and served. Clement of Alexandria brought into Christian theism the philosophical absolute which has played havoc with it ever since. Augustine carried over the notion of the absolute from the category of substance to that of will with devastating results. The Pantheists and the Deists and the dualists have all made their contributions, so that it is often difficult to discover anything distinctively Christian in our so-called Christian theism.

But there are two forms of theism that may fairly be recognized as Christian, for they exist only within Christianity. The first is Trinitarianism. There have been trinities in other religions but nowhere else this particular Trinity—the Father, the Son, who was incarnate in Jesus Christ, and the Holy Spirit. Whether the Trinitarian theism of the Christian church is essentially as well as formally different from other and non-Christian theisms depends on the character of the triune God. Sometimes the recognition of Christ as the incarnation of the second person of the Trinity has introduced schism into the character of God, the Father being thought of as righteous, the Son as merciful. This of course is a polytheistic and genuinely pagan conception. More often the deification of Christ has had no effect whatever on the character of God. Christ has been read in terms of God—the infinite, the omniscient, the omnipresent and so on—rather than God in terms of Christ. The Trinity in this case has been only formally not really Christian.

An essential element in the historical doctrine of the Trinity was the Logos Christology. The Logos was a philosophical device for mediating between God and the world, or between divine transcendence and divine immanence, and its inclusion in the godhead under the name of the Son left God to all intents and purposes just what he would have been were there no Christ or

Christianity. Adequately to serve its purpose, I may remark in passing, the Logos should have been identified with the Father instead of the Son, but Christian apologetic made the latter identification necessary, to the hopeless confusion of the whole matter. While the triune God then is formally a Christian God, accepted only within Christian circles, he may or may not be really so.

On the other hand, any theism may be regarded as genuinely and distinctively Christian, whether it be Trinitarian or Unitarian, when it interprets God in the light of Christ or when it makes God Christlike. God is not read deliberately and consciously in such terms except among Christ's followers. Here then we have a distinctively Christian theism and I am inclined to think there is no other theism entitled to the name.

It will perhaps be claimed by some that Christian theism is the theism taught by Jesus, and that his message about God should be taken as determinative. But as a matter of fact Jesus taught Jewish theism exclusively. The God he worshipped and served was the God of his fathers and of his countrymen. He introduced no new features into the picture of him, nor did he modify in any way his people's thought of God.[1] Even when he spoke of God as Father, as the Jews had long done, it was of God's sovereignty he was chiefly thinking. The common notion that he emphasized the love of God more than the Jews were in the habit of doing is not based on his own teaching as reproduced

[1] For Jesus' thought of God see, further, McGiffert, *The God of the Early Christians*, pp. 3–21.

in the Synoptic Gospels but on the writings of Paul and John.

In the sayings of Jesus recorded in the Synoptic Gospels there is no explicit reference to God's love, though it appears frequently in the Gospel and First Epistle of John and in the letters of Paul, as well as in the Old Testament and contemporary Jewish writings. The two assumptions that Jesus went beyond his countrymen in speaking of God as Father and that he used the word Father particularly to indicate God's love and mercy are both erroneous. The term Father for God is common among most peoples as it was among the Jews. In earlier Jewish literature it was employed chiefly of God's relation to the Jewish people, but before the time of Christ it had come to be employed also of his relation to individuals. When used it did not commonly involve affection solely or even chiefly but ownership and authority. But in Jesus' use of the word and in that of his countrymen it was as a rule synonymous with other names for God and interchangeable with them. "The Most High" is kind toward the unthankful (Luke 6:35); the Father acts as judge (Matt. 10:33); prepares eternal fire (Matt. 25:41); punishes the unmerciful (Matt. 18:35), and so forth.

It should also be noticed that Christ says surprisingly little about divine forgiveness and that in referring to it he seems interested rather to warn his disciples against presuming upon it than to strengthen their belief in it. Of course I do not mean to imply that Jesus did not believe in God's goodness and kindness and

mercy and forgiving love, as a good Jew he could not
have done otherwise, but only that all this was but a
part of his thought of God, and that he did not go beyond contemporary Judaism in the matter.

To Jesus as to the Jews in general, God was the
one and only God; the God of Israel and of all the
world besides; an almighty being able to do anything
however impossible, with a perfect knowledge of all
things including the future; the creator and ruler of
the world who controls everything in the most minute
way, making the sun shine, the rain fall and the grass
grow; who watches over sparrows; who cares for men,
feeds and clothes them, numbers the hairs of their
heads, fixes their destinies, even leads them into temptation, and in general can do whatever he pleases with
them. He is also the judge of all the earth who rewards the good and punishes the wicked; a God to be
feared and yet to be loved, severe in his punishments
and yet merciful and gracious to those who repent and
turn to him, and full of unmerited kindness to both
good and evil. He is at the same time a holy God whose
interest, however, as maintained by the great prophets,
is less in the cult than in moral righteousness and goodness, and whose holiness does not set him apart in such
a way that he cannot be found by those who seek him
and cannot be seen by the pure in heart. All this is
genuinely Jewish and represents no new conception of
God at any point. If we are seeking for a distinctively
Christian theism we cannot find it in Jesus' teaching
about God but in Jesus himself, his life and character

and purposes. In other words, the Christian God is not the God of Jesus, the God whom he worshipped and served, but a God like Jesus.

But what does this involve? It is to be noticed in the first place that Jesus sharpened the Jewish law: Except your righteousness exceed the righteousness of the Scribes and Pharisees; he that is angry with his brother shall be in danger of the judgment; he that calls him a fool in danger of hell fire; he that looks on a woman to lust after her has committed adultery with her; do not use oaths; do not resist him that is evil; turn the other cheek, give up your cloak to him who takes your coat; go the second mile; love your enemies; forgive without limits; keep your good deeds to yourself and pray in secret not in public; judge nobody; lay not up treasures on earth; at the judgment you will have to render an account even for idle words; be undivided in your allegiance, hating even your father and mother. If the Christian God be like Christ he must demand such conduct of those that worship and serve him.

Again, Jesus was very severe in his judgment of evil and very stern against evil doers: If your eye or your hand offend you, pluck it out or cut it off. Not every one that saith unto me Lord, Lord shall enter into the kingdom of heaven. Many will say unto me in that day, Lord, Lord did I not prophesy in thy name? and then will I profess unto them I never knew you, depart from me ye workers of iniquity. He condemned not only the wicked husbandmen but also the foolish virgins and the man without a wedding garment. He told the twelve to shake the dust off their feet against any community that did not receive them, and that it would be more tolerable in the day of judgment for Sodom and Gomorrah than for such a community; and he said the same thing about Capernaum and other cities which did not repent at his mighty works. He declared that there should be taken away from him who hath not even that which he hath; that he would deny before his Father in heaven those who denied him before men; that the wicked should be cast into hell fire; that it were better for a man to be thrown into the sea with a millstone round his neck than to cause a child to stumble; that only those who forgave others should be forgiven and that blasphemy against the Holy Spirit would never be pardoned, though the Jewish doctrine was that every sin whatsoever shall be forgiven him who repents. He called the Pharisees blind guides, offspring of vipers, fools and hypocrites, and he pronounced terrible woes upon them as well as upon the scribes and the lawyers. He called his own generation evil and adulterous, faithless and perverse; he said to Peter "Get thee behind me Satan"; he cursed the barren fig tree, and cast out the money changers from the temple. Evidently if the Christian God be like Christ he must be severe in his judgments and stern against evil doers.[2]

On the other hand, Jesus was full of love and kindness and mercy and compassion, helping everybody that needed help in every way he could, healing the sick, not simply forgiving but helping the sinful, interested

[2] The need of such an emphasis today is apparent. There is too much sentimental palliation of evil.

even in the humblest and meanest. There seemed no limits to his sympathy and helpfulness, for he was come to seek and to save that which was lost; though to be sure his mission was only to the lost sheep of the house of Israel, not to those outside. In spite of this, he healed the daughter of the Syrophœnician woman in response to her appeal. The Christian God then must be like Christ in these respects too.

But it is not enough that the Christian God should have a character like Christ's; he must be one in purpose with him. For it was not simply that Jesus loved his fellows and was eager to do all he could to help them; he endeavoured to make them, too, loving and kind and helpful. It was his definite and deliberate aim to bring his disciples into right relations with their fellow men. He had much more to say about men's relations to each other than to God. To have the right attitude toward one's brethren *is* to have the right attitude toward God. This it may perhaps be said is what he meant by the kingdom or reign of God.

With what insistence he dwelt upon the matter! "Thou shalt love thy neighbour as thyself." How seriously he took this Old Testament injunction and how broadly he interpreted it is shown by the parable of the Good Samaritan. Love your enemies, pray for those that despitefully use you and persecute you; be good to all, the evil as well as the good, the ungrateful as well as the grateful; be perfect in goodness even as your Father in heaven is perfect; sell all you have and give to the poor; forgive even unto seventy times seven;

whosoever will be great among you let him be your minister; and perhaps most striking of all the judgment scene in Matthew 25, in which not his attitude toward God or Christ but his treatment of his fellows is made the one test by which a man stands or falls.

There can be no possible doubt that the Jesus depicted in the Synoptic Gospels was supremely interested in promoting the spirit of love and sympathy and service among men, and if the Christian God be like Christ he too must be supremely interested in this. It may fairly be claimed that this is what the love of God should be interpreted to mean if we are talking about the Christian God, a God like Christ. Not that God wishes to make all men happy as the rationalists maintained, not that there is in infinite being a propensity to diffuse itself, as Jonathan Edwards held; or that God desires to impart himself to men and to arouse in them the consciousness of their oneness with him as Schleiermacher taught; but that he would have men truly brothers. As Ritschl puts it "Therein that we in the kingdom of God love our brethren is the love of God realized."

Finally it is not enough that the Christian God should be like Jesus in character and purpose, he must be read also in the light of Jesus' service and sacrifice: the Son of man came not to be ministered unto but to minister, and to give his life a ransom for many; I am among you as he that serveth. And his devotion was such that he did not stop even at the cross. There is no sign that Jesus read God in such terms. Jew as he was, with his thought of God as almighty creator and sovereign, he could hardly have read him thus. But we must read God thus if we are to make earnest with our principle that the Christian God is like Christ. In the mystery-cults of the ancient world much was made of the figure of a dying and risen deity. Whether or not the wide-spread belief in such redemptive deities had anything to do with the Christian belief in a suffering and dying and risen Lord, at any rate the beliefs are akin.

But if the Christian God is to be like Jesus, it is not sufficient to confine the suffering to Christ even though he be the incarnation of the second person of the Trinity. God, himself, must serve and spend and suffer for the good of men. Whether the doctrine of the atone-ment be accepted or not, an essential part of Christian theism, and I am inclined to think the most distinctive thing about it, is the belief that God's purpose to build the kingdom of love and sympathy and service among men stops at nothing, even at suffering and self-sacrifice.

If God be thus interpreted in the light of Christ's life and character and purposes, he may properly be called a Christian God whether he be identical with the God Jesus worshipped or not. There are elements in such a God that are lacking in the God of Jesus and there are elements in Jesus' God that may be lacking in the Christian God. If God be read in terms of Christ he is a Christian God, even though he be not, as Jesus thought him, the almighty creator and ruler of the world. Of course the belief in divine creation is not in-consistent with Christian theism, but it is not essential to it. Our principle of differentiation makes a serving and saving and self-sacrificing God necessary, but not a creator God or a God of physical power.

It is perhaps worth asking what are the validating grounds of faith in such a God as I have described. We may if we please reach faith in a creator God by the old cosmological and teleological arguments, and in a providential ruler of the world by the study of history. We may gain first-hand assurance of God's existence by the experience of mystical communion with the divine, if that be possible to us. On the other hand, the road to a knowledge of the Christian God is the road of Christian service. I am not aware of any other way of proving the Christian God. If men live as if the Christian God were, and living thus find life increasingly satisfying and are conscious of growing victory, they may gain an assurance as real as the mystic's own. If now and in all the ages to come the hypothesis that there is such a God works; in other words, if it vindicates itself in our experience and in the experience of those of our fellows who also believe in him—if it vindicates itself, that is, in our common social experience—there can be no completer proof that he is.

Chapter XIV

COMMUNION WITH GOD

There is first the mystical conception of communion with God in the thoroughgoing form of oriental and neo-Platonic mysticism which involves ecstasy and finally the complete losing of oneself in God. The closer the communion the more one loses consciousness and will, and the ultimate is the complete extinction of individuality.

Serious objections may be brought against this conception: in the first place it is philosophically unsound in that it involves the pressing back of all phenomena to a noumenon quite unmediated in experience; in the second place the end which it contemplates, namely the losing of one's consciousness in union with the divine, means that God or the absolute is ultimately the same as nothing; and finally it is utterly unchristian in that it operates wholly with the metaphysical category of substance and sacrifices altogether the personality of God.

Closely related to this conception is another of much greater interest to us because very common among Christians of today—the idea of communion with an immanent God; or with the universal spirit immanent in the world and in man. Every man is supposed to be potentially one with the infinite and to commune with

God is simply to open one's nature to him and let the infinite universal spirit take possession. Consciousness of the infinite or of the absolute is the favourite phrase. Immediacy is the quality of the relation—"Nearer than hands or feet" is a popular expression of it.

It is liable to objections similar to those urged against the first conception. It is ontologically unsound in that it involves the getting back of phenomena to the noumenal. That one may assume a noumenon back of phenomena is of course true, but that one can hold valid communion with it—that one can press back beyond phenomena and come into direct touch with it is a delusion. And then again nothing could be farther from Christ's conception of God than this; for it means the substitution of a metaphysical abstraction for the personal God and Father. It should be said also that with this conception of communion it is impossible to distinguish between reality and hallucination. What guarantee can we possibly have that we are actually communing with God and not with our own imaginings?

In the third place there is the common anthropomorphic conception, in which God is pictured as an individual with whom we can hold converse back and forth— much as a child with its doll. And even where the anthropomorphism is less crass, the conception remains essentially the same when it involves the idea of an interchange of confidences—or of a conversation between God and ourselves such as might take place between friend and friend. This view has one great advantage in that it makes God distinctly personal;

but it is beset with the serious and indeed fatal difficulty that there is absolutely no means of distinguishing it from hallucination. The tests of reality cannot be applied to it and so there is no certainty that it is a valid communion in any sense.

Communion in all these cases means passivity more or less complete: in the first case it means contemplation, ecstasy and finally complete loss of individuality; in the second case a more or less hazy and indistinct exaltation or uplift of spirit similar to the inspiration which a poet receives in contemplating nature; in the third case it exhausts itself largely in intimate and friendly converse with a supposed divine companion.

The true Christian conception

In order to reach this we must ask what have we given us as Christians? We have a personal God, the Father of Jesus Christ, whose purpose is revealed by Christ. This God has come to our knowledge through Christ and having learned to know him in looking at Christ we recognize his activity in the world, in the church and in our lives. His purpose we see is fulfilling itself ever more fully in the world and in the church and in ourselves as Christians. We have not looked upon this Christian God, we cannot picture him in any visible form but he is a person, for he has a definite purpose and he is consciously labouring for its accomplishment and our Christian faith means recognition of the purpose as revealed in Christ and belief in its ever fuller accomplishment; that is, belief in God's goodness and his power. But beyond this recognition of God's purpose and its increasing accomplishment we cannot penetrate. To try to get to a being back of the purpose is vain. Of course, purpose involves being but for us the being expresses himself in the purpose and to a being unexpressed we cannot penetrate any more than we can penetrate through phenomena to an unexpressed Ding-an-sich, and come into immediate touch with it.

To commune with God then is to enter into his purposes as revealed in Christ—to make them our own and to fulfill them increasingly and to gain the inspiration and the power which come from knowing that they are God's and will be increasingly fulfilled and will ultimately prevail. Genuine communion with God to the Christian is the conscious and glad fulfilling of God's purposes. It is an active not a passive thing.

It may be carried on in passive moments as one reflects on the purpose of God and gains inspiration through such reflection but true communion is reflection or contemplation not for its own sake but always for the sake of the better fulfilling of the purpose. The moment it loses this active reference it ceases to be communion with the Christian God, for his purpose as revealed in Christ is active purpose for us and we commune with him only as we enter sympathetically into his purpose and so make it our own. The completest communion is active service in the conscious recognition of God's purpose. Communion with God is therefore not something divorced from Christian service, a different end and ideal—a parallel employment of the

Christian life—so that a man may commune *or* serve or commune *and* serve; the two are *one*. We recognize God's purpose and believe in it and give ourselves to its accomplishment. Our recognition of it and our belief in it and our devotion to it we carry with us all the time, both when we are actively serving and when we are not. To say that when we are actively serving we are not communing and vice versa is to mistake our true relation to God altogether. We cannot be always actively serving in the very nature of the case. If we could it would be a fuller realization of communion with God than is now possible to us. Many say that seasons of communion are necessary in order to serve and that the service should purposely be stopped in order to give such seasons. This may or may not be so. I have my doubts about it; but it is true, of course, that thoughtful intelligent service with the constant recognition of God's purposes is better and truer service than blind thoughtless activity.

Still further it is true that there must in the very nature of the case be seasons of cessation from activity and that such seasons may be better spent in contemplating and drawing inspiration from God's purpose than in empty thoughtlessness or absorption with something quite different. In other words, whether active or in repose, the more constantly the consciousness of God's purpose is with us and the more unbroken our devotion to it the more completely shall we fulfill it. If some find they cannot think while they are active and so need the quiet seasons of contemplation in order to become aware of God's purposes, of course I should advocate the quiet seasons for such men, but I should wish to insist that they are truly communing with God when they are actively fulfilling his purposes and that such quiet meditation as they crave is not the only communion with God nor indeed the highest and completest form of communion. If it is genuine communion at all it is so only in so far as it has to do with God's purposes and looks toward the actual fulfilling of them.[1] So I should wish to insist that worship both public and private should have as its sole purpose the better-fitting of the worshipper for the fulfilling of God's purposes, that it should not be thought of as an end in itself or as having any other end whatever than preparing for active service.

If my interpretation of communion with God is correct, it is clear that communion with the living Christ as distinguished from God is not possible. As God is known to us only as purpose and as Christ's purpose is identical with God's, as he is himself the historical embodiment of it, we cannot distinguish between God and Christ in communing with the divine purpose. All attempts to do so are foredoomed to failure and simply encourage the substitution of fancy and hallucination for reality.

[1] A somewhat different interpretation was given on a later occasion [Editor]: "Let me speak first of my own experience of constant prayer. I pray constantly, asking God for anything and everything, telling him all my desires and ideals and plans. I do not pray for spiritual things only. That means too much rationalizing of prayer; and prayer is not a thing to be rationalized. We should rationalize doctrines, but not attitudes. Prayer is an attitude and a temper. The advantages of such praying are that it keeps my desires high and unselfish and subject to God's will. The consequence of such praying is that I do not observe special seasons of praying any more than of breathing and loving."

Again, it is clear since we have learned to know God through Christ we can know him now only in the light of Christ; that is, only as the purpose which Christ expressed. To attempt to go beyond the historic Christ and to discover more of God than he revealed, that is more of God than is expressed in the controlling purpose which he revealed, is vain. And so to talk about new revelations of God if we mean by it revelations in any way either contradicting or transcending the revelation made by Jesus is to talk vanity, for the purpose of God revealed by Jesus is supreme and cannot be transcended; on the other hand if we mean larger knowledge and fuller understanding of God's purpose as revealed in Christ we may have ever new revelations, as through study of Christ and our own experience in service we learn more and more of the fullness of the meaning of God's purpose.

Various objections may be brought against the conception of communion which I have presented. It may be said for instance that I make of it a very impersonal matter—a purpose being given the place of a person. To this objection I should reply that purpose is the very essence of personality and that God is known to us only as a purposeful being. Of God unpurposeful— of God over and above purpose—I at any rate know nothing. I know only an active God. That "God *is* love" for instance means to me only that God has for me and for others a purpose of good. I might *imagine* a passive love—or depths of character, as we say, in God back of and beneath his purpose, but I can *know*

nothing of them. It is God as *purpose* that is revealed
to me and into the depths of the unrevealed God, if one
were to imagine there were any such, I could not penetrate. Conscious fulfilling of God's purpose is communing with God himself, a personal God, in the full-
est sense.

Again it may be objected that I make of communion
an altogether external and objective thing. But this
objection means, I should say, that the objector is still
in the grip of the old ontological mystical conception of
religion. As compared with oriental theosophy and
neo-Platonic mysticism Christianity is external and objective if one chooses to call it so, and the communion
with God which it inculcates cannot be of a different
character. How great was the emphasis laid by Christ
upon active service! How little he had to say of passive
contemplation! There is not a word of the latter in the
Lord's Prayer and hardly a word in the Synoptics. To
try to bring into a religion which makes active service its
ideal a conception of communion taken from religions
which have an altogether different ideal is to injure
Christianity and to obscure its real significance.

Once more, it may be objected that I am disregarding
altogether the testimony of Christian experience in
interpreting communion with God as I do; that to make
communion simply the conscious and glad fulfilling of
God's purposes is to throw out the testimony of Christians of all ages who have testified to their own experience of much more than this as the most precious experience of their lives. In reply to this I may say that to

build our conception of genuine Christian communion with God upon such experience without the most careful and rigid questioning of the experience is most precarious. It is like building our ontology on the testimony of the common man that material things are *real in themselves*, because everybody sees and touches them. I venture to think that as far as there has been genuine communion with the Christian God—and I believe there has been much in all the ages—it has meant sympathetic entrance into his purpose and conscious fulfilling of it; and that when the experience is carefully questioned this will be found to account for the inspiration and help Christians *have* received from their communion, so far as such inspiration and help have been really divine.

This leads me to a final word about the reality of the kind of communion I have been talking about as distinguished from the other kinds referred to at the beginning. The reality of this communion with God is as certain as the reality of the Christian God himself. If the Christian God is, I certainly commune with him when I consciously and gladly fulfill his will. But even given the Christian God we can never verify our communion with him if communion be taken in any other sense than this. We can never know whether it is really God or our own imaginings we are communing with at any time, and it is just because of this that there is so much unreality in our common talk about communion.

In conclusion I may call attention to the apologetic value of my conception of communion. We may all the time increase the testimony to the reality of the God we have learned to know through Jesus Christ by our experience and the experience of others in fulfilling his will, but for the validity of other kinds of communion we have no guarantee and upon experiences of such communion consequently we can build no guarantee of the reality of God himself.

SECTION C

THE CHRISTIAN LIFE

Chapter XV

THE CHRISTIAN FREEMAN

The apostle Paul was a radical, the first and greatest radical in Christian history. In the opinion of most of the early disciples, his contemporaries, the institutions of Judaism were of permanent validity and were to be retained intact in the Christian community. Christianity was to be a religion of repression, binding men to the observance of a rigid moral and ceremonial code and restraining them from doing what they would naturally like to do. Against this Paul protested in the strongest terms. "Where the Spirit of the Lord is, there is liberty." Paul was hated and persecuted by his fellow countrymen both within and without the circle of disciples but he won his battle and Christianity sloughed off the old system in which it had its birth and a genuinely new religion was the result. To be sure it soon fell back again into the bondage of legalism. Fearing that Christians would not think and live as they ought unless subjected to the pressure of law the church elaborated its own doctrinal and moral code, not identical with that of the Jews, but in principle the same. Assuming men's natural propensity to evil it strove by all sorts of prohibitions and inhibitions to repress their natural impulses and desires and to keep them from being themselves.

With this religion of repression the reformer Luther broke completely, as Paul had broken with Judaism, and started Protestantism on its career as a free religion of the spirit. But the old distrust of man proved too strong for it and it soon fell back again into the traditional rôle of a moral police. In these modern days we are coming to see that this is a low view of the function of religion; that there are plenty of influences making for human bondage and repression and that religion ought not to be one of them, but ought rather to set men free and to open before them the large liberty of children of God.

I want to consider religion as a liberating influence: not something that restrains men but that sets them free; not something by which they are cramped and circumscribed in their thinking and living but by which they are broadened and enlarged. Of course the other view of it is still very common. The professing Christian is widely supposed to be prohibited from doing many things he would like to do and which his neighbours have no compunctions about; and they often pity him for the deprivations to which he is subjected. I wish it could be everywhere understood that there is nothing he wants to do which the Christian is prohibited from doing; that the Christian is not under law but is a free man in Christ Jesus, and that if he abstains from doing this or that it is because he does not wish to do it, because his heart is set on something else. The liberty which such a man enjoys is not that of the jail-bird who has broken out of his cell and roams at large a hunted thing and still a criminal at heart. It is the liberty of one who does not need to be controlled, for he controls himself, who does not need to be bound by law, for his character and conscience are his law. He lives for high and holy ends, not because he is commanded to do so but because it is his nature to. This is what Paul meant by Christian liberty. The man who has the spirit of Christ needs no law to make him do right and keep him from doing wrong. He does the right and eschews the wrong of himself. It is his joy to live in the spirit of Christ. His religion does not bind and limit and repress him; it is a creative force within him, finding glad and eager expression in a life of purity, of generosity and service. I wish it could be everywhere understood that religion is really a liberating force and that its essence consists not in closing but in opening doors, not in restraining but in setting free.

I do not mean by religion its trappings and adornments—rites and ceremonies and rituals—its embodiment in organization, its formulation in creeds, its external symbols—church and synagogue and temple—but the spirit of reverence, the attitude of worship, the consciousness of the divine, faith in God and devotion to his will. Religion in this sense is not confined to Christianity, but most of us know it only in its Christian form. Whether in Christianity or in other cults it is the heart of the matter, and it is with its influence in setting free the spirit of man that I wish particularly to deal.

Let us look then at some of the things from which

and to which religion frees us—or would free us if it were properly understood.

For one thing it frees us from the dominance of material things. We are bodies as well as spirits and we have much in common with the lower animals from whom we are descended. In comparison with the long ages, five hundred thousand or a million years perhaps since man has been upon the earth, it is but a short time since he emerged from barbarism and entered upon a civilized existence, distinguished from that of the brutes chiefly by the growing dominance of mind over body. Civilization has not advanced by denying the body and despising material things. The ages of asceticism retarded rather than promoted the growth of the human spirit. But civilization has advanced by making the body the servant of the mind instead of its master and material things tools instead of tyrants.

Among the forces that have dignified the spirit of man and made it conscious of its rightful heritage none has been more potent than religion. During many ages it was the one influence that gave men assurance and enabled them to assert their superiority to the things that surrounded them. Now that that superiority has been established for many centuries the race can get along without religion better than it once could. But it still remains the highest expression of man's spiritual consciousness. As he comes into touch with the divine his lordship over the world and his birthright as a free creative personality become most manifest to him.

It is this consciousness of freedom that enables us to take the right attitude toward material things. We cannot do without them. To despise them is folly; to turn our backs on them suicidal; but to let them take possession of us and control us is to sell ourselves into slavery. Material things have their place, but a strictly subordinate place. They are a means to life; they should never be its end. As Thoreau once said, "I do not go to the woods to get my dinner, but to get the sustenance which dinners only preserve me to enjoy." To make bodily pleasure or comfort, to make the pursuit of wealth or any other material things the end of life is to belie ourselves as spiritual beings and to sink to the level of the brutes. Not asceticism, contempt for material things, but the use of them for higher ends, this is the part of true wisdom.

Release from the dominance of material ends is needed particularly by those who are labouring in our day for economic and political reform. It is folly to think a new and better world can be secured by simply improving the physical conditions of life. Such improvement is sadly needed without doubt, but more is necessary if permanent advance is to be assured. Not merely shorter hours and more humane surroundings, but a better understanding between capital and labour and a keener sense of social obligation on the part of both; not merely a reduction of armaments—naval and military—but a better understanding among nations and a keener sense of their responsibility for the common good of all. There are those who confine their efforts to the improvement of physical conditions because these alone seem important. As a matter of fact no improvement in physical conditions can possibly be lasting without a change of mental attitude and of spiritual atmosphere. There are those who confine their efforts to the improvement of physical conditions because this alone seems practicable and attainable. But it is no more practicable and no more easily attainable than an improvement in mental attitude and in spiritual atmosphere. We should not confound the latter with the vain dreams of those who expect the speedy coming of the millennium. Because we realize that brotherhood is not going to prevail immediately between individuals and classes and nations everywhere, that the world is not going to become perfect all at once, there is the more not the less reason why we should labour to promote mutual good-will and to infuse improved material conditions with a better and more humane spirit. It is the spirit that giveth life. It alone has creative power. With it anything can be achieved in time; without it nothing of permanent worth.

I have said that religion frees us from the dominance of material things. It frees us also, or it ought to free us, from narrowness and pettiness, from prejudice and partisanship. It seems almost ridiculous to make such a claim as this. When we recall how often religion has been the fruitful source of bigotry, when we think of religious sectarianism and remember the countless wars that have been fought in religion's name it seems like

irony to commend it as a liberator from prejudice and
partisanship. But surely it is a primitive and unintelligent form of religion that narrows the mind of man
and circumscribes his sympathies. A polytheist who set
his god over against the gods of other peoples might
have ground for partisanship, but how faith in the one
God and Father of all men can contract man's outlook
and shut him off from his neighbours it is hard to see.
Of course it could not were it really understood and its
implications recognized.

If religion means anything at all it means the worship of a being greater than ourselves. A being confined as we are, with no wider outlook and no larger
vision, could not possibly be the object of any intelligent man's adoration. The God we worship must be
exalted above the barriers that hem us in and must see
vast stretches of life that are hidden from us. To come
into communion with such a God, to endeavour to think
his thoughts after him, and to put ourselves in sympathy with his purposes ought to broaden us and raise
us above the petty limitations that beset and confine us.

In these days particularly religion should serve as a
uniting force among all the nations of the earth. A narrow and exclusive Americanism, like any other narrow
and exclusive nationalism, is essentially irreligious. It
is not necessary that the whole world should be Christianized, or that all nations should embrace a common
belief, in order that religion may become a uniting instead of a dividing force. However diverse the faiths
of men, religion should diminish the causes of friction

and bind peoples more closely together as it lifts them to a loftier point of view, widens their horizon, and enlarges their sympathies. The religious man may properly try to spread the light he has and to impart to others the ideas and ideals he cherishes, but as a worshipper of the one God of all the earth he can dare to do so only in a spirit of sympathy and appreciation, with full recognition of the rights of others and of the legitimacy of their faiths and convictions.

Whether church union comes or not, or the union of all the religions of the earth, is a matter of minor concern; but that unity of spirit shall everywhere prevail, that bitterness shall be outgrown and mutual recrimination abandoned, and that Christians of differing sects and men of various religions shall learn to live together in harmony and to co-operate for the common good of all—this is absolutely essential. To this, if they but knew it, the religious men of all the world are committed by their very faith in God and devotion to his will.

Again religion frees us, or ought to free us, from bondage to the past. To be sure it is often thought that bondage to the past is one of the things for which religion has been chiefly responsible. We are reminded over and over again that because of its devotion to old ideas and ancient dogmas the Christian church long opposed the advance of modern science, and that it is still in many quarters a sinner in this regard. But to charge this to religion is to misunderstand its true nature. It is not religion nor is it Christianity that is responsible for such obscurantism but the weakness of the human mind and its natural dread of change. Religion if it be living and vital can be content only with a living God, the kind of God Christ meant when he said, "God is not the God of the dead but of the living." With such a God we may well expect daily evidences of his presence and daily revelations of his will and truth. To declare that God communicated with men centuries ago but has never done so since is to relegate him to an outworn past. It is no wonder the age-long prevalence of this belief made God seem to multitudes as good as dead and promoted the widespread conviction that our modern world can get on perfectly well without him. There has been indeed no more fruitful source of atheism. True religion on the other hand finds God here as well as there, now as well as then. While it may recognize that God was revealing himself in other days as men were able to understand him, it is very sure at any rate that he is revealing himself now. In the daily experience of fellowship with him the religious man finds the real basis of his faith and confidence. This makes him not the slave of the past but its master. Instead of testing the present by the past he tests the past by the present. He does not despise the past and treat it with contempt, as many modern radicals are doing, for he believes God was there as well as here; but the only way he can be sure that this or that ancient revelation came from God is by discovering in it the character and spirit of the God he knows and worships. And hence he is not the blind devotee of the past as many conservatives are. He uses the past; he is not controlled by it. He does not demand that the present shall harmonize with the past before he will recognize its truth. By its own evidence it must fall or stand.

One of the most difficult problems in any age is rightly to adjust ourselves at once to the past and the present. The conservative is bound by the past; the radical breaks with it and will have nothing more to do with it. Both are equally at fault. By neither is wisdom shown. Past and present are not enemies or competitors; they belong to one undivided stream of time. The wise man is he who recognizes the continuity of old and new; who has eyes for the true and the good whether discovered in other ages or in our own. Particularly in these days of change, when all existing beliefs and institutions are falling under criticism, it is well to acquire this sense of continuity. To be hostile neither to the old because it is old nor to the new because it is new, but to be hospitable alike to both and eager to learn from both what they may have to teach, this is the part of wisdom.

Again religion frees men from fear, one of the most enslaving passions of the human mind. Anthropologists tell us that primitive man was a creature subject to the most devastating fear—fear of nature, of unseen demons, of wild beasts, of fellow men. The growth of civilization and the advancement of science have robbed the world of most of its terrors. The forces of nature we have harnessed to do our bidding; invisible demons we no longer believe in; wild beasts we have tamed or banished from our neighbourhood; and we have learned to live as a rule on decent terms with our fellows both of our own and other races, except when temporary insanity overtakes us and we revert for a season to the barbarism of war.

But fear still binds the human spirit and keeps it from living in the perfect freedom it is fitted for; fear of death which casts a constant shadow over the lives of many; fear of the future which prevents them from facing life bravely and adventuring boldly; fear of the unknown and the untried which enslaves them to the familiar and conventional and makes all progress impossible. From all sorts of fear religion should free a man. With faith in God whose child he is and whose world this is he ought to be able to face death without a tremor and the unknown and the untried with confidence and equanimity.

Science has not banished danger from the universe. It has discovered or invented countless forces pregnant with destruction of which our ancestors knew nothing; electricity, radium, dynamite, TNT. The world is full of dangerous things. But we do not go about in constant dread of them for we have learned how to transform them from enemies into servants. Similarly religious faith does not banish danger from the universe. Death is still here, and new and unfamiliar experiences face us both in present and in future, experiences often to try men's souls. But we are not demoralized by them for we see in them divine providences, or means of grace, or opportunities for service. Religion teaches us how to make instruments of them and to use them for good ends instead of being overcome and vanquished by them.

Religion releases us also from fear for the cause of truth and righteousness—a fear that often paralyzes effort and reduces us to timid apologists when we ought to be victorious champions. No doubt religious faith has sometimes been a substitute for human effort. Believing in God men have sometimes left everything to him in the fatuous confidence that he would do whatever was needed and that all would be well with the world whether they did their part or not. But this, of course, is to fall back into the primitive and childish belief in magic. As science does not present us with natural forces which we can trust to do our work without co-operation on our part—like the fabled genie of Aladdin—but with forces that must be directed to the ends we would achieve, so religious faith does not give us a God who will bring in the kingdom of justice and brotherhood and peace independently of us and without effort of ours but a God who works in and through us and our fellows, illuminating and inspiring us to do what needs doing and what without us and them will never be done. If we believe in the ultimate victory of truth and righteousness—that the kingdom of God will yet come upon this earth—it is not because we expect God to bring it about by the exercise of his

miraculous power, but because we are confident that his
divine purpose will increasingly gather to itself the devotion and the sacrifice of the worshippers of God and
the lovers of their brethren, and will make them strong
to conquer and achieve.

I have enumerated some of the things from which
religion sets us free. The list might easily be length-
ened, but I have said enough to indicate what I mean
when I speak of the liberating influence of religion. It
is that aspect of it I have wished particularly to emphasize because to so many it appears in the guise of a
jailer shutting us in behind closed doors, and shutting
us off from much that is best and most alluring in life.
Religion is not necessary in the sense that food and
drink are necessary. A man can live and thrive if he
wants to without it. Religion is not a duty in the sense
that virtue and service are duties. A man may be good
if he wants to without it. Religion is a privilege. It
strikes the shackles from man's spirit and opens to him
higher levels and broader skies than otherwise were his.
It liberates within him impulses and desires which else
were dumb, ideals and aspirations which else were un-
discovered. It sets free unsuspected powers. It not only
makes weak men strong, vile men pure, selfish men
generous, timid men brave, but to the best and the
biggest it opens opportunities of spiritual experience
and of human service that challenge all that is biggest
and best within them. In its atmosphere flourish faith
and hope and confidence and trust—those attitudes

which sweeten life, which make the world fairer, and promise the coming of a better day. In its atmosphere the noxious weeds of fear and distrust, suspicion and jealousy wither and die. For religion means freedom not for the worst but for the best. Not where prejudice and faction and selfishness and greed are, but where the Spirit of the Lord is—the spirit of understanding and sympathy and service—there is liberty.

Chapter XVI

THE CHRISTIAN TEMPER

Faith and hope are our privilege. Love is our duty: "Thou shalt love."

The genuine Christian attitude undoubtedly includes both faith and love. The true Christian believes in God as well as loves his neighbour. Faith as opposed to doubt and fear was one of the chief emphases in Jesus' teaching. But when the lamp of faith burns low, when all goes wrong and hope gives way to despair, no Christian is excused from doing his duty, from labouring for the things he knows are right.

We must never make the mistake of measuring our duty by our faith. There are certain things that ought to be and we must labour for them when we despair of their achievement as faithfully as when we are sure of it. Undoubtedly, speaking generally, the accomplishment of great things depends upon the belief that they are feasible. But they will never be accomplished if they are striven for only while their feasibility is evident. They must be striven for when the outcome is doubtful as well as when it is sure. I suppose labour for the rescue of the outcast rests ultimately on the belief that rescue is possible. But he will not undertake such work who confines his effort to those he is confident of saving.

The kind of temper that leads men to fight hardest

when the fight is going against them is the kind of temper that is needed in Christian service. To let our labour wait upon our faith, to fight well only when assured of victory, is to betray the cause we fight or labour for. It was a profound insight of Kant's that led him to reverse the ordinary maxim, "I ought because I can" and to say "I can because I ought." Faith can wait upon love, but not love upon faith. Our duty we *must* do whether it eventuates in success or in failure. We may well hope for a confidence never shaken and never clouded in the victory of the Christ we serve and follow, but we shall hardly deserve the victory until we have faced the alternative and have learned to say in all sincerity: "Better to perish with Christ than to reign with Cæsar."

Chapter XVII

FORGIVENESS

The sentimentalism that wants everybody bad and good to be happy has no place in an ethical religion like Christianity. Christianity has commonly been spoken of as a gospel of forgiveness. This is to misunderstand Christianity. Its gospel is rather one of reformation and righteousness: the kingdom or rule of God.

In his teaching Jesus represented God not as an easy-going, good-natured deity, but as a stern and severe God. God's standards are high. He is very hard on sinners. Christ was more severe than the Pharisees, not less so. He was an Amos calling for Reformation. He had very little to say about divine forgiveness. He was interested rather to warn his disciples not to presume on it. What he was interested in was the forgiveness of one's enemies. This was in protest against selfishness, an over love of self. By this he did not mean the forgiveness of other people's enemies. That is only a form of moral weakness. It is not ethical at all. It is possible only because we care too little about other people, about those who are hurt.

We have no right at all to forgive any enemies but our own. Christianity is not mere general good-nature or kindliness. We may win an enemy by forgiving him, for such forgiveness costs us something. But we do nothing to win a man when we send some one else the second mile with him, or give him some one else's cloak, or forgive him when he has injured some one else, not us. Forgiving another man's enemy costs us nothing. Such forgiveness is a kind of moral indifference. It helps nobody, though it may make a man feel more comfortable, when in fact he ought not so to feel.

I venture to say that even God has no right to forgive some one else's enemy. Nor should a man seek divine forgiveness for an offense against some one else than God. In the Lord's prayer we pray for forgiveness for offenses against God. These are many and various: irreverence, indifference, disobedience, and so on. But to ask God to forgive us for our offenses against another man is unsound. It is the other man whose forgiveness we need, not God's.

Asking divine forgiveness for all our sins comes from the notion that all our sins are sins against God. As a matter of fact it has been commonly thought that to interpret all sin as sin against God is to increase its gravity and to give us a keener realization of its awfulness. But I fear it does not always work that way. As a rule we would rather humble ourselves before God and ask his pardon than before our fellow men. And so far from heightening our sense of sin by making God instead of men the offended person such procedure is apt to diminish it. Otherwise there is no harm in the notion that all sin is sin against God, though it is apt to smack of artificiality, unless—as I have remarked is too often the case—divine forgiveness is substituted for human forgiveness. Then it is indeed bad. We have no right to ask God's forgiveness until we have asked it of our offended brother; and we have no right to accept God's forgiveness as a substitute. Nor, it should be added, have we any right to ask forgiveness of our brother until we have made reparations. Mere repentance is not enough.

The truth is that divine forgiveness is commonly another phrase for self-forgiveness. If we think divine forgiveness easy it means we are easy with ourselves, and this is ethically demoralizing. We should never forgive ourselves. The peace of mind got through penance is ethically bad, not good. The idea that we are forgiven and all is as if it had not been gives a peace of mind that is to be deplored, not praised. We can outgrow our sins but not forgive them.

Christianity interpreted as a religion of forgiveness has done much to soften our moral fibre. It has led men to think that they can escape the consequences of their sin, whereas, in fact, they cannot escape them. The doctrine of divine forgiveness is the corollary of the doctrine of divine punishment. God inflicts eternal punishment upon the wicked and, having inflicted it of his own will, he may remove it on any conditions he pleases; as the Pope may grant indulgences on any conditions he pleases. But we modern Christians do not commonly interpret the sufferings of the wicked in this way. They are the natural consequence of sin, not God's infliction of punishment. Even God himself cannot remove them. Forgiveness cannot help. Having changed from a legal to a natural interpretation of the divine activity, we ought not to retain the legal notion of divine forgiveness.

To be sure the modern emphasis on forgiveness is only natural. It is a reaction against Calvinism and Puritanism. But it is unwholesome none the less. The notion that sin can be done away by forgiveness is wrong. So far as sin is an act it cannot be done away by anything. So far as sin is a disposition or attitude it can be removed only by being replaced by a different disposition or attitude. The antidote for sin is not forgiveness but righteousness. If the Catholic is wrong in his supposition that forgiveness can be earned by penance, the common Protestant notion that repentance brings forgiveness is still worse. Jesus, it should be noted, nowhere connects repentance with forgiveness except in Luke, as for example, in the story of the Prodigal Son. Neither penance nor repentance is the opposite of sin. In the case of an offense against our fellow we may repent and ask him to forgive us. If he is a Christian he will do so freely. But we ought not to forgive ourselves and no one else ought to forgive us until we have made full reparation, or until we have become righteous. It is not forgiveness we need any way. We need reformation, which, of course, includes reparation. Too often the preaching of forgiveness stands in the way of the demand for righteousness.

In the light of this discussion about the nature of forgiveness, we must inquire about the Protestant doctrine of salvation which makes it synonymous with forgiveness and makes forgiveness absolutely free to the believer. Let me remind you that for Luther himself forgiveness or salvation was simply in order to service. Where one is kept from serving others or from doing his duty to his fellows, as Luther saw many were by fear of the divine wrath, then one needs forgiveness and may be given the full assurance of it by any Christian brother. Such forgiveness is not meant to free him from sin but to set him free to service. Forgiveness is intended to free men not from irreligiousness but from over-religiousness.

Thus understood the Protestant doctrine of forgiveness is unobjectionable. It gives man liberty to serve. But forgiveness for any other purpose is both vicious and unprotestant. To preach forgiveness now when it really means as it so often does setting a man free from serving his fellows rather than to serve them is altogether wrong. What is really needed by a sinner is not forgiveness. He should be educated away from that idea; and we should be, too. The sinner needs moral impulse and power. What reforms a man is not forgiveness—the condoning or belittling of his faults— but trust, the belief of another person that he can be better, and his example to make him want to be better. Sometimes because of existing ideas self-confidence cannot be gained until one believes oneself forgiven. In such a case let a man believe it. But educate him out of the notion that forgiveness is what he wants, when his real need is for moral incentive and strength.

This impulse and this moral power, according to

Christianity, can be got from Christ. The revelation of Christ and of the kingdom of God for which he lived may lay hold of a man and create moral impulse. Forgiveness after all is but negative and Christianity is profoundly positive. Men are saved by Christ, not by being forgiven, but by being given a new purpose which itself creates new moral power. As Christians we should talk to the wicked man not about forgiveness but about opportunity, not about wiping out the past—that he cannot do—but about making the future splendid and glorious. Christianity is the gospel of the kingdom, a forward-looking faith.

CHAPTER XVIII

THE SECOND MILE

Jesus did not say, If any man compels you to go a mile, 1. compel him to go another; 2. stand upon your rights and refuse to go; 3. go the mile cheerfully; 4. go with him the full distance, leaving not a rod untravelled; but rather, 5. go with him two. The first mile is the mile of duty. The second mile is the mile of free service. When you have done all you are requested to do, then do more.

Thus Jesus added the principle of love to the principle of law. This principle finds such ready application in the home and among friends that it is unnecessary to re-enforce it with illustrations. Yet it can and should also be applied in the wider and less personal relationships of business and politics. For note that the principle of the second mile does not mean love instead of justice; not the second mile instead of the first, but in addition to the first. The first must not be neglected; the second comes after it. And as a matter of fact social, political, and business history are full of examples of the going of the second mile. Once slavery was thought to be necessary; child labour, long hours, and unhygienic conditions in shops and stores, low wages; any means were justified to win victories in the competitive struggle. But now many things which were

formerly simply ideals for some men have become
duties and we have to observe them. We condemn practices our fathers approved. We are in fact going the
second mile continually. The glory of this principle is
that it contains the secret of all moral progress. The
mile of freedom becomes the mile of law or duty and
then we go on to farther miles of freedom and so we
grow in moral stature personally and socially. For morality is not something static. It is constantly changing
and developing as the voluntary becomes the required.

The principle of the second mile applies not only to
love and service but also to faith. There are those who
say, like W. K. Clifford, Believe only what you are
obliged to believe; believe only what is proved to be
true. But others, like William James, insist on believing all they can; on being hospitable to the unproved.
The former had rather risk the loss of truth than the
chance of error; the latter, however, think it better to
risk the chance of error than the loss of truth. They
make the venture of faith. Only as we advance beyond
the first mile of knowledge and go on to the second mile
of faith is progress possible either in science or in religion. This does not mean that we shall substitute
faith for knowledge. Faith is not credulity. It means
that we shall supplement knowledge by faith.

Many people, quite apart from Christianity, have
acted on this principle of the second mile, but according
to Christianity God also acts on the same principle.
Christianity's greatest gift to the world is that of a God
who goes the second mile continually with his children,

who treats us far better than we deserve, going beyond the demands of justice, causing his sun to shine and his rain to fall on the evil as well as on the good; bringing good out of evil and overruling us to our benefit. His perfection consists in his doing more than he is compelled to do, even to the loving of his enemies and doing good to them that hate him. Many are the gods of justice and law and duty but the Christian God is the only God who acts on the principle of the second mile.

God is so quiet and unobtrusive about it all. So many people are self-conscious and disagreeable and insufferable in going the second mile, traversing it superciliously or self-righteously, until we hate them for their very virtue. Life is full of such complacency and conscious rectitude. In contrast with this attitude is the unobtrusive goodness of God, who even hides himself so that we do not see him unless we look for him. To go the second mile quietly and without ostentation, as naturally and as simply as the sun shines and the rain falls, even when no one knows it, without thought of credit or merit or praise—this is to live Christianity, this is to be perfect in the same measure as our Father in Heaven is perfect.

Chapter XIX

THE SENSE OF PROPORTION

In the multiplicity of interests and occupations too many of us draw no distinction between the more important and the less. Everything makes equal demands upon us and we fritter away our time and strength on whatever happens to turn up until we lose the power of concentration and of effective service. Or it may be we confuse the values of life and devote ourselves heartily and steadily enough to things of lesser worth, as the Pharisees once devoted themselves to the tithing of mint and anise and cummin. We are troubled with myopia and need to have our vision readjusted. We need to recover the sense of proportion. Because of their nearness the small things look large and the bigger things lying beyond and above them are lost sight of altogether. Even a low wall, scarcely higher than our heads, may hide from us rich prospects of nearby park and distant mountain.

The endless and meaningless round of tasks and pleasures, how it obscures the real values of life! how it paralyzes thought and aspiration! Our ceaseless coming and going, the ceaseless motions of our hands moving things hither and thither, the ceaseless opening and shutting of our mouths in empty talk, how they fill our time and absolve us from the duty of doing anything worth while, of living for ends that really count.

But of what sort are the ends that count? Of what sort are the things worth living for and living for supremely?

It is evident enough that things that simply fill up time are not worth spending time upon, things whose significance ends with the doing of them and whose claim to recognition rests upon the fact that they have occupied the time employed in doing them. I suppose the greatest economist of the ages will be he who learns how to turn to the profit of society the vast areas of time now thus wasted by the race!

It is evident also that the support of life is not itself fitted to be the supreme end of life, and yet—sometimes, to be sure, under the demoralizing stress of economic pressure, but often because of mere blindness or empty-headedness—the support of life is treated as if it were an all-sufficient end, and what is done with the life thus supported is taken as relatively immaterial. Could anything be more fatuous?

It should be evident also that mere pleasure, whether it be of a lower or a higher order, physical, æsthetic, intellectual, or spiritual—temporal or eternal—is not fitted to be the end of life; for pleasure is simply an accompaniment, a concomitant of living, and to regard it as its end is like taking the oil that lubricates a machine as the end for which the machine exists.

Indeed we may go farther and say that nothing that stops with the doer of it is fitted to be the end of life. No man lives unto himself alone. He must not, it is true, be used by others as a mere means to serve their ends—this is a fundamental principle of ethics—but as a member of the human family the end of his existence is larger than himself, and to make himself his own end is like making a machine its own end. Nothing indeed exists for its own sake alone; everything points without and beyond itself and takes its meaning from a larger whole. The worthy ends of life then are to be found always beyond the confines of our own personal interest. Whether that interest be health, or pleasure, or well-being, or fame, or wealth, it is not big enough to be any person's chief aim.

The transcendence of self may be as it were spacial, or it may be temporal as well; the service of those about us or devotion to a cause that continues after we are gone. Some degree at least of amplitude and some degree of permanence every end must have if it shall be worthy the supreme endeavour of a rational being.

Such amplitude and permanence need not characterize the things we do in pursuance of our end: they may be of the humblest and simplest kind. The end we do it for may glorify the smallest as it may degrade the greatest deed. It is in the end we make our own, not in the means we employ for its achievement, that our sense of proportion chiefly displays itself. Take, for instance, the common tasks done in the workshop by the man who is earning daily bread for himself and his family, or those done in the home by the wife and mother, the demands upon whose time and strength never cease. To live worthily is not necessarily to do

other and greater things than these. The situation may
be such that there is neither time nor strength for anything else. To live worthily is to do the things that
must be done, however humdrum and commonplace,
with a worthy purpose. Interpreted in the light of life's
real values, the tasks we have to do cease to be small
and insignificant. They take their character from the
motive that prompts them. It may be the overmastering sense of duty, it may be the welfare of dear ones,
it may be the pursuit of truth or the advancement of the
world's store of knowledge, it may be the service of
God. Done for any worthy end the tasks we have to do
cease to be mere mint and anise and cummin and become themselves the weightier matters of the law—justice and mercy and faith. Only when they degenerate
into meaningless routine, as the ox and the ass go un-
thinkingly their daily round of toil, only then does the
soul as it were drop out of them and they become the
irremediably little things, too mean to absorb the time
and strength of a human soul.

Justice and mercy and faith, how often they are
crowded out, not by love of injustice, cruelty, and false-
hood, but by absorption in other and lesser things! The
movement for political reform, how often it is blocked
by party regularity; economic and social advance by
class prejudice; the redemption of the world by the
inability of Christians to rise above their denominational
loyalties and co-operate unreservedly in a common task.
Not wickedness but blindness is the great curse of the
world; not viciousness but the lack of a sense of pro-

portion; not love of evil but devotion to the *lesser* good.

The sense of proportion may be understood to mean recognizing the supreme values of life, so that we devote ourselves to matters really worth while instead of wasting time and strength upon things that do not count; or it may be understood to mean estimating accurately the value both of the greater and the lesser things, so that we attend to the former while not neglecting the latter. It was this sense of proportion Jesus once urged upon the Pharisees. He would have them do both the big and the little things, not allowing the latter to take precedence over the former or the former to crowd the latter wholly out of sight.

If there are many who draw no distinction between the greater and the lesser things of life, there are others so alive to the overmastering importance of certain great ends that all else seems as nothing to them. Giving themselves with commendable devotion to a single and it may be a highly worthy object they deliberately or unconsciously close their eyes to all lesser things. This way doubtless lies the temptation of the trained and serious-minded man and woman. Success in this or that enterprise has been gained by concentration and concentration comes to seem the only law of life. But this also is to violate the true sense of proportion. Concentration there must indeed be—persistent labour for definite ends—but there should also be an open vision for all life's values and opportunities. Many a family suffers from a lack of this sense of proportion on the part of one or another of its members. There are men highly successful in business or profession whose families are entirely deprived of their society and who themselves are bereft of the humanizing influence of the home simply because they are too enslaved by profession or business to think of anything else. Young people too are sometimes afflicted with the same kind of blindness. In their praiseworthy zeal to get an education and fit themselves properly for the responsibilities of life they turn their backs—sometimes when they should not—upon the home duties and interests, sacrificing what seem to them the smaller for the larger values, or it may be, so absorbed in the latter that they wholly overlook the former. I would not imply, of course, that devotion to particular ends—business or profession, public service, the gaining of an education—is not commendable. On the contrary, as I have already said, no life is worth while unless it be organized for some definite purpose that commands our allegiance and enlists our best powers.

But is it possible to give ourselves adequately to the accomplishment of any end and to achieve real success in it without turning our backs upon everything else?

In reply I should say it depends upon what the end is. I can well believe, as an eminent banker once said about the amassing of great wealth, that there are certain ends which can be compassed only by the person who sacrifices everything to them, literature and art and recreation and friends and love and domestic joys and service of his neighbours. But success in such a case is too dearly bought, and reveals a deplorable lack of a true sense of proportion. A really worthy end will not—ordinarily at any rate—demand this particular species of devotion; a worthy end will broaden and enrich, not contract and impoverish character. If it cuts a person off from all the other values of life, if it narrows one's horizon and circumscribes one's interests, if it tends to make one less of a personality and more of a machine, it is not the sort of an end that any real man can afford to devote himself to. The only things worth living supremely for are large and inclusive things. As we ascend a mountain the view gradually broadens and embraces an ever-widening prospect. So as we follow upward the scale of life's values we find them growing steadily broader and more inclusive. At the bottom are those that concern ourselves alone, our own selfish welfare and enjoyment. The person who lives for them grows steadily blinder to the better things of life. Then come the values that have to do with those nearest and dearest to us. How one who lives for these is carried out of oneself and finds one's own joys multiplied and one's own life elevated and enriched! We are not ourselves excluded from the larger circle of values—we expand to its dimensions. Similarly as our vision widens to include the community, the nation and the world. Rightly understood these are not exclusive but inclusive. Not the family against the individual, the community against the family, the nation against the community, and the world against the nation. In every case the larger circle includes the smaller. We rightly serve the world, the nation, the community, the family, not by eschewing the smaller group but by including it in our ministry. To recognize the claims of both, the larger and the smaller, and to make the service of each contribute to the good of the other: this is the part of true wisdom.

There was a time when people thought to serve God by cutting themselves off from all lower things, from all the interests and concerns of common human life; when religion meant forgetting one's neighbours in order to remember only one's creator. For many a century it was believed that family love and the delights of friendship were incompatible with the highest piety because tending to distract the mind from love for God; and so monasticism became the supreme Christian ideal. Now we see that this meant a fatal loss of the sense of proportion and a sad distortion of the true values of life. We have learned to read religion in a larger way, and we know that piety and devotion to God are best exercised not apart from the world but in and through it, that we are nearest to God when closest to his children, and that we serve him best in serving them. Interpreted thus the service of God is fitted to be the supreme end of life, for it is inclusive not exclusive, and enriches rather than impoverishes. Devoted to the eternal and the infinite we need not be blind to the temporal and the finite, for the former does not contradict the latter but includes it. Part of the eternal and the infinite as it is, nothing that is temporal and finite is alien to one who is aware of God and lives for him. A religion that thus broadens and enriches life is the only religion fitted to enlist our supreme devotion, and if we be blessed with a true sense of proportion we shall find any narrower and smaller faith intolerable.

Human progress, the progress of the race as a whole, depends upon the conservation of old values as well as upon the creation of new ones. To draw an illustration from history: the individualism of the eighteenth century, in which tendencies culminated that had their birth in the Renaissance, marked an undoubted advance upon the corporate emphasis of the Middle Ages, when the individual was too generally subordinated to the authority of church and state. In its reaction against the past, however, the eighteenth century emphasized the supreme worth of the individual at the expense of the community. Its conception of society was atomic in the extreme, and values were sacrificed that could ill be spared. The nineteenth century endeavoured to do justice both to the community and to the individual. Its great watchword was unity, but this meant not a return to the barren uniformity of an earlier day but rather the attainment of a richer and higher unity. Not sameness—a dead level of conformity—but the harmony of many diverse elements. This is what modern democracy means, or ought to mean. Freedom and independence for all, but at the same time the willing devotion of all not to their own separate and divisive interests but to the general good.

The supreme social value is a commonwealth of free persons. A mutual relationship of parts to whole and whole to parts characterizes every genuine organism. The parts are not ends in themselves, but means to a larger end, and yet the larger end is itself in turn not mere end but means to the being and well-being of the parts. Only in it do they have their existence as only by them does it exist.

What then of the relation of the larger to the smaller ends of life? It is all a question of preserving the proper balance, a difficult thing at best and demanding a large share of wisdom. To know what is truly worth while; to know when to give oneself exclusively to one thing and when to give to other things their due share of attention; he who has learned this has learned the fine art of living and has discovered the secret not of usefulness alone but of happiness as well. It is not an affair of rules and formulas. There are no absolute and unvarying standards. The values of life are relative. To estimate them justly is the task of the wise man. We have to do it at our own risk. We may blunder and in giving ourselves to the wrong things make shipwreck of this life of ours, or in trying to be fair to all its interests we may become fragmentary and ineffective. But if we are alive to the situation—if we try to keep an open vision for the true values of life—we shall grow in wisdom and it may be we shall ultimately gain such a sense of proportion as shall lead us unhesitatingly and inevitably to choose aright; for after all the highest kind of living is not that which is always governed by calculation, and consists in laboriously weighing one value over against another, but that in which the response is immediate, spontaneous, and free. We may then fairly define the wise man as he who instinctively knows the true relation and proportion of the values of life, the smaller as well as the greater; and the good man as he who fulfills the injunction of Christ: "These ought ye to have done and not to have left the other undone."

CHAPTER XX

THE PLACE OF THE SACRAMENTS IN PROTESTANTISM

The traditional Catholic theory of the sacraments, which is as old as Cyprian, and which has its roots in the teaching of the apostle Paul, I need not dwell upon here. According to that theory the sacraments are mysterious and sacred rites, "which not merely symbolize or signify an inner sanctification of man, but actually effect it." They are efficacious signs of divine grace in that they "really effect the grace which they signify." (I quote in both cases from standard Roman Catholic dictionaries.)

The theory is based upon the belief in the corruption and depravity of the natural man, which render him liable to eternal destruction and make it impossible for him to escape from it until he has been transformed by divine power. This corruption being conceived in realistic fashion, as it was both in east and west from the time of Irenæus on, the divine influence, which brought the transformation, was likewise conceived realistically, and the sacraments became means—and ultimately the only means—whereby a divine substance known as grace was conveyed to the recipient. The sacraments might be called, as they were by Augustine, and as they are in the Catechism of the Council of

Trent, "visible signs of an invisible grace," but they are always more than mere signs. They actually "contain the grace which they signify," according to the Council of Trent, and by means of them that grace is actually conferred upon those who partake. In spite of minor obscurities, the Catholic theory as a whole is clear and consistent and constitutes an integral part of the Catholic system.

On the other hand in Protestantism the doctrine of the sacraments has been beset with confusion and uncertainty from the beginning, and under the circumstances it was impossible that it should be otherwise. In substituting an ethical for the traditional physical conception of salvation, and in maintaining that salvation consists in divine forgiveness, not in the transformation of human nature, Luther repudiated the basis upon which the sacramental theory of the Catholic church was built; but unfortunately he retained the sacraments themselves, or at any rate two of them, because he believed they were commanded by Christ. It became necessary therefore to reinterpret them, and this he did when he asserted that they are merely signs or testimonies of God's forgiving love in Christ and that they have exactly the same sort of efficacy that the spoken word of the proclamation of the gospel has; that they are in fact merely the word made visible. This reinterpretation was in line with his reinterpretation of the word grace, which he took to mean not something to be given or conveyed to man but simply God's gracious attitude or forgiving love. Our word graciousness ex-

presses better than our word grace the meaning of grace
as Luther wished to have it understood. This view of
grace was entirely consistent with his notion of salvation
and of course with such a view it was impossible to think
of the sacraments as conveying grace. Strictly speaking
there was no grace to be conveyed. They *could* be nothing more than signs of God's graciousness.

But this interpretation of the sacraments broke down
even in Luther's own hands when he came to deal with
the particular sacraments of baptism and the Lord's
Supper. The retention of the rite of infant baptism
made the first difficulty. If baptism was to have any
value at all to the infant baptized, it seemed necessary
to make it something more than a sign or testimony,
which could have no value unless accepted in faith. The
result was that Luther was driven to talk about baptism
in the traditional way, as the sacrament of regeneration.
In other words he made it a means of imparting a
supernatural substance or influence, which wrought a
change, not in the affections or dispositions or will of
the recipient, but in his nature or φυσις.

Akin to this was the effect of the notion that Christ
is truly present in the eucharist. His words, "This is
my body," as they had originally given rise to the belief
in the real presence, seemed to Luther to necessitate
the retention of the belief, and he was the more un-
willing to let it go, because it constituted so strong and
striking an evidence of the forgiving love of God in
Christ of which the eucharist was itself a sign and testimony. But the belief made almost inevitable the recog-

nition of the eucharist as something more than a mere sign, and it is not to be wondered at that Luther himself came to think of it in the old way as the food of the regenerate nature, and as actually imparting a supernatural something to the recipient. This view of the eucharist—like the view of baptism just referred to—early became practically universal in Protestantism both Lutheran and Reformed. That Luther believed in the material presence of Christ in the eucharist while Calvin and the Reformed wing of the church generally talked about a spiritual presence is a matter of minor consequence. All insist that Christ is truly present and that the believer truly feeds upon him and thus the eucharist is something else than a sign or testimony of "the forgiving love of God in Christ." It is a sign and testimony of Christ's presence, which is an altogether different matter, and it is more than a sign and testimony even of this for "worthy receivers"—according to the Westminster Confession—"outwardly partaking of the visible elements in this sacrament, do then also inwardly by faith, really and indeed, yet not carnally or corporally, but spiritually, receive and feed upon Christ crucified"; or as the Heidelberg Catechism puts it: "with his crucified body and shed blood he himself feeds and nourishes the soul to everlasting life as certainly as I receive from the hand of the minister and taste with my mouth the bread and cup of the Lord."

It is significant of the influences operating in this connection that in many of the Protestant confessions the general statement of the doctrine of the sacraments is more Protestant than the particular statements about baptism and the Lord's Supper. In almost every case the two are made more and other than mere signs or testimonies of "God's forgiving love in Christ."

But lying back of the traditional interpretation of baptism and the Lord's Supper—which was taken over in essence by the reformers—and affecting far more than the mere theory of the sacraments was the traditional doctrine of original sin, which all of the Reformers retained, and to which they gave a fundamental place in the Protestant system. Concerned as Luther was to destroy all idea of human merit, and trusting only in the free grace of God in salvation, he emphasized the doctrine of human corruption and depravity as it had hardly been emphasized since the days of Augustine. Luther's attitude in this respect was adopted by Zwingli and Calvin as well, but thereby a fatal inconsistency was introduced into Protestant thought which has been a fruitful source of confusion ever since.

When Luther identified salvation with forgiveness he was moving wholly in the ethical realm—the realm of personality—but when he talked about original sin he was in another realm altogether. The notion of original sin is strictly physical, not personal or ethical. When any one talks about an inheritance of sin or native corruption or depravity, he is going back of the individual affections and volitions in which alone the ethical has its abode and is dealing with physical and non-moral conceptions. The consequence is that it becomes necessary for him to think, just as the Catholics have always thought, of a transformation of man's nature or φύσις. Mere forgiveness is not enough; there must be regeneration as well. And ever since Luther's day orthodox Protestant theologians have been trying to combine satisfactorily the Catholic notion of regeneration with the Protestant notion of justification quite without success, for the two notions are entirely disparate. The one is physical, the other personal and ethical. Retaining the traditional notion of original sin, and the consequent need of regeneration or the birth of a new nature, it is not to be wondered at that Protestantism retained the traditional notion of the sacraments. If this be Protestantism, then sacraments in the strict sense as vehicles of supernatural grace effecting regeneration and nourishing the regenerate nature are in place in Protestantism as truly as in Catholicism.

But many modern theologians believe that this is not genuine Protestantism. At any rate they are sure it is not genuine Christianity; and if Protestantism has not yet been truly Christian they are anxious to make it such. They maintain that Christianity, as given to the world by Christ himself, is strictly ethical, that it has to do with personal relationships and personal character, not with physical or metaphysical entities. Therefore they are trying to ethicize the Protestant system of theology through and through and to get rid of the old pagan physical conceptions which the Reformers took over from Catholicism.

Where the ethical conception of Christianity prevails there is no place for sacraments in the traditional sense of that term—no place, that is, for means of grace which are addressed to a non-ethical, non-personal nature or substance, supposed to constitute the substratum of human life. Means employed to affect or control such a nature belong in the category of magic, however spiritually they may be phrased. We should not be deceived by the sounds of words. We are apt to take for granted that the term spiritual means ethical and personal over against the material and impersonal. But, as a matter of fact, throughout Christian history it has also had another meaning as far from the personal and ethical sphere as the conception of matter itself. And wherever a spiritual presence of Christ in the sacraments is talked about which makes them any more than mere signs or testimonies or appeals to the mind and heart, there the word spiritual is used in this physical non-ethical sense, and we are as truly in the sphere of magic as any Roman Catholic with his doctrine of transubstantiation.

What then should be the attitude of the modern Protestant to the sacraments? Must he, in consistency, repudiate them, or may he continue to observe them with a good conscience? If he believes that Christ instituted them and commanded their continued observance I suppose he may feel compelled to retain them even though he finds himself out of sympathy with them. But if he believes as I do, on grounds which I have given elsewhere and cannot repeat here,[1] that Jesus instituted neither baptism nor the Lord's Supper, he will be perfectly free to judge them solely on their merits.

If I thought that their continued observance tended to

---

[1] See McGiffert, *The Apostolic Age,* pp. 68 *ff.*

promote the old non-ethical idea of Christianity, then I for one, much as I am attached to them, should think it far better to give them up altogether and to rely for inspiration upon other and more strictly ethical means. And if the orthodox doctrines were generally held, I do not see how they could fail to promote that idea. For whether Catholic, Lutheran, Anglican or Reformed, that doctrine is at bottom the same, and is neither ethical nor Christian.

But so far as I can discover, comparatively few Protestants, at any rate in Presbyterian and Congregational churches, are really orthodox on the subject. To most of them apparently baptism, if it has any meaning at all, is simply a ceremony of dedication or consecration, and the Lord's Supper a memorial of Christ or a token of our Christian fellowship. If this be all they are, I can see no harm in them, and I can understand, indeed I know, that great inspiration and good may come from their observance.

But three things seem to me important. In the first place, we ought to be diligent to reinterpret them for our people and to ethicize them through and through. In the second place we ought to cease calling them "sacraments." The word has historically a very definite meaning and to continue to employ it when that meaning has been repudiated not only tends to deceive others, but also exposes us to the constant danger of the return of the old physical and non-ethical conceptions for which the word historically stands.

In the third place I believe it should be made clear to

all the people that we do not regard participation in either ceremony as essential to membership or good standing in our churches. We condemn the Baptists for requiring immersion in order to church membership. We are just as much to be condemned if we require baptism. The one is no more *necessary* than the other. Let us continue to observe the rite, which has a peculiar beauty and significance—especially when given to infants—but let us not *require* it. Also let us make our members clearly understand that attendance upon the Lord's Supper—beautiful and inspiring as the ceremony is—is equally optional and is required of *no* Christian and of *no* church member.

In these ways the modicum of misunderstanding that still attaches to the two ceremonies—if there be any misunderstanding of them left today in our churches—may be overcome, and the two rites do all the good they are fitted to do and none of the harm they have sometimes done.

CHAPTER XXI

VISION

I sometimes think that the Book of Revelation, with all its obscurities and difficulties, its inexplicable symbols and unsolved riddles, is one of the most significant books of the Bible, for it is wholly made up of visions, visions seen by John when he was in the Spirit; and what is Christianity but a vision of the invisible, brought to bear upon the duties and responsibilities and trials of the daily world of sight and sense? Jesus began his ministry with the words, "Repent, for the kingdom of Heaven is at hand," an immediate duty based upon the vision of an unseen reality. And what was all his teaching but lessons drawn from his visions of spiritual things hidden from the eyes of the multitude?

There can be no doubt that much of the significance and abiding power of all religion lies just here. In every religion there is contact with a higher world, from which is drawn inspiration or comfort or strength. If the daily round of toil or of amusement were enough, if the soul found full satisfaction in it and craved nothing higher and more enduring, if the common life were its own adequate explanation and furnished its own sufficient ideals and inspirations and energies, there would be no need of religion. Man is religious because he is more than a brute, because he lives in a world higher than that of sense, because he thinks, and longs, and plans, and hopes, and cherishes ideals. "Where there is no vision the people perish." Religion is the fruit of man's search for a vision that he perish not. Even the most ignorant heathen who worships wood and stone worships them not for what they are in themselves but for what they symbolize. Through them he gets in some mysterious way a vision of an unseen world, of unseen forces playing about him, upon which he can rely or which he needs must fear. No one worships the mere thing he sees but always a something unseen, felt indeed but not visible to the bodily eye.

Why is it that in spite of the discoveries of modern science, leading to such changes in our views of the origin and growth of the universe, in spite of our break with many of the old dogmas, in spite of the fact that we count as the rankest superstition much of the religion of the past—why is it that in spite of all this we are still religious, still frequent the house of God, and engage in the customary services of worship? It is not a mere matter of custom. It is something much deeper. It is due in part at least to the longing for a vision, that this daily life of ours, much of it so meaningless and valueless if taken by itself alone, may be given significance and worth. Often we seek in vain. The service seems empty and barren. The preacher has only threadbare tales to tell, rumors of visions seen by other men in other times long gone, but we keep on in hope, and every once in a while directly to our own hearts, as we bow in prayer, or through the word read or spoken, comes a new glimpse of the reality and glory of spiritual things, and the whole week is illumined for us. The daily tasks are performed with unaccustomed zest and the daily sacrifices made with unwonted joy. Linked up anew to God our lives seem again in some degree divine, and fresh confidence and courage fill our souls.

The vision is often sought as an escape from the humdrum monotony or the racking misery of our daily life, as one seeks distraction at a play. But it is the distinction of religion that it opens to us not the vision of fleeting unrealities, gone as soon as seen, but of abiding realities in whose light all we are and do is transfigured and, it may be, transformed. It is not alone that weakness craves strength and depression craves inspiration, but that the human soul, too large and too lofty for the petty and passing things of sense, craves room to be itself, and to know itself for what it is.

There never was a time when men needed visions more than now. Without them it is impossible to withstand the pressure of the feverish pace of modern life, the multiplicity of occupations, the mad rush for wealth, the dominance of materialism, theoretical and practical, the World War which brought almost to bankruptcy our boasted civilization, with its cherished moral and spiritual values; and now the narrow provincialism, the petty partisanship, the greed, the suspicion, the anarchy that are abroad among us. It is impossible to face the disasters and to measure up to the needs of the present unless we have a vision of higher and better things to stay and steady us.

There are many kinds of visions, empty fancies, beautiful, if you please, but out of all relation to life. Some of the visions of the seer of Patmos were of that character. Such visions concern us not. There have been too many of them in the history of the church, and there are perhaps too many of them now—too much seeking after them and too much absorption in them to the detriment of more important interests and often to the promotion of discord and strife. The visions needed today are not of that sort, not mere idle fancies, but great realities lying before us and summoning us to make them actual.

The secret of Christ's permanent hold upon the world is largely this, that he saw visions loftier, more compelling and more enduring than those seen by other men before or since. He saw for one thing a vision of God; not a great impersonal power, an unreasoning and conscienceless fate, but a Father by whom even the hairs of our head are numbered and without whom not even a sparrow falls to the ground. "Fear not therefore, ye are of more value than many sparrows." Into a world of oppression and tyranny in which the poor were ground down by the rich and the life of no humble man was safe, in which all the powers of nature and of man seemed leagued to terrify and crush, Jesus brought the vision of a divine Father who careth even for the meanest.

In preaching the gospel of deliverance from sin we have sometimes forgotten that Christ preached also deliverance from fear. It is the great glory of Christianity, and the boast especially of Protestant Christianity, that it teaches trust. In trust is found the secret of salvation, indeed the very sum of salvation, salvation from fear of God's wrath, from fear of men, from fear of the world and sin and death. The gospel of freedom which Christ preached, and the reformers after him, was primarily a gospel of liberation from a life of anxiety and dread into a life of serene confidence, a gospel based upon the vision of the divine Father in whose hands are the destinies of the whole race.

Jesus saw, again, a vision of the possibilities of humanity. Looking upon the outcasts of his day whom every orthodox Jew thought corrupt and accursed, he detected in their faces the lineaments of his own Father whose children they too were; and sublimely confident in the power of the gospel of divine forgiveness and love, he summoned them to be perfect even as their Father in heaven was perfect. What faith in man, matched only by his faith in God! With his vision to inspire them and urge them forward those who toil for the redemption of humanity need never despair.

And then Christ's vision of the kingdom of God. In the midst of the injustice, the unholy ambition, the thirst for world dominion, the wars of aggression and of oppression which disfigure the history of the Roman Empire, to dream of a world in which love and righteousness and justice and peace should reign—was ever dream bolder than that? A dream it was, but it has already in some measure transformed the western world.

The abolition of slavery, the spread of democracy, the theory at least if not the practice of human brotherhood, the common recognition that equal justice and equal rights and equal opportunities should be enjoyed by all, the growing conviction that each man is his brother's keeper, if much of all this remains still unrealized it is at any rate a compelling ideal for an ever-increasing multitude of men, and the time will yet come when the vision will be an established fact, and this world of ours will actually become a holy place, the kingdom of God in which dwelleth righteousness.

It was one of the sources of the tremendous power of the early Christians that they saw the vision not merely of a heaven lying far away beyond the grave but of the kingdom of God established there and then. They were mistaken. It took longer to transform the world than they had dreamed. As a consequence the vision faded and was replaced by that of a heaven in some distant star and the social power and pressure of the early faith were largely lost. Even so, the vision served to comfort the hearts of multitudes and to quicken and purify their lives. Now seen again in these modern days as Jesus saw it—a new world wherein dwelleth righteousness—it lays upon us a new responsibility and challenges us to new endeavour.

Men crave big tasks. Not for things of little worth but for great ends they rejoice greatly to suffer as well as greatly to labour. We forget it often. We think that everybody lives instinctively for selfish gain or selfish ease. But a great crisis like war comes upon us, and we find men quick to sacrifice all they hold most dear. It is not that men love to fight, though doubtless many do, but that in what seems to them a high and holy cause even men who detest fighting rejoice to fight and men who dread dying rejoice to die. The trouble with peace is that it too seldom offers glittering opportunities for suffering and sacrifice for a great end. Opportunities enough there are, God knows, but not commonly of a type to arrest the imagination and compel enlistment.

Christianity itself, since the early days when the martyrs stained red the soil of Asia, Africa, and Europe with their blood, has too often worn the aspect of flowery and inglorious ease. How trivial the demands it makes! A decent life, membership in a respectable church and attendance upon its services, and the expenditure of a few petty dollars annually for its support! And people wonder that Christianity is not more of a success in the world! What is there to arouse enthusiasm in a religion thus interpreted? We ask little and few bother to give anything. We ask the impossible and multitudes spring to the challenge. If the thing be only big enough, that it seems impossible—we might almost say—is the surest warrant that it will be done.[1]

The actual transformation of this world of ours into a world of righteousness, of justice, of sympathy, of brotherhood, of mutal service—was there ever a bigger and a harder thing proposed? Is it because it seems too hard that multitudes are not throwing themselves into it? Nobody who knows this humanity of ours can

[1] The curse of the ancient world into which Christianity was born was the deep-rooted conviction, shared by upper and lower classes alike, that to the great mass of people the doors of opportunity were altogether closed, that aspiration and achievement were only for the favoured few. Jesus came preaching the eternal worth of every human soul, declaring even the humblest to be children of God, and summoning all men, low and high alike, to labour and suffer and die in the service of the great ideal. And Christianity swept the Roman world.

imagine it for a moment. It is because the multitudes have not caught the vision of it. To most men it is a mere empty dream, a form of words, a pious platitude. It is not by making it seem easy but by making it seem real that the devotion of the world is to be enlisted.

The imagery of the closing chapters of the Book of Revelation, the walls of jasper, the streets of gold, the gates of pearl, probably makes little impression on most of us today. The trouble with it is not simply that we have outgrown the imagery but that we take it to refer only to heaven, whose foundations we cannot lay, and whose walls we cannot build. If we but saw the vision of a holy city here on earth, with its walls builded by us and by those who come after us, the vision would be a challenge to the best that is in us and them; and it would not forever remain a mere vision, but by the striving and the toiling and the suffering of those who saw it it would be translated by and by into actual fact.

CHAPTER XXII

CREDO QUIA ABSURDUM

One of Christopher Morley's delightful little books contains this striking sentence: "The difficulty with ecclesiastical creeds is not that they are too hard to believe but too easy." I have often felt that one difficulty with Christianity, as currently interpreted, is that it is too easy, that it does not demand enough of a man, and seems to many not worth while. Perhaps this is true also of our creeds. It may be that they are too tame and commonplace, that they contain much that is not interesting or does not matter even if it be true.

"Credo quia absurdum." I believe because it is absurd. There is something in human nature that responds to those words of Tertullian. We want to believe the unexpected, the unbelievable thing. We want to be adventurous in our faith as well as in our deeds. When our existing creeds were made they were adventurous enough. To ask men to believe in God the Father Almighty, when they had known only the petty gods of Greek and Roman myth; to ask them to believe in Jesus Christ, not only dead and risen but coming again to judgment, when they had known only Dionysus or Attis or Adonis or Serapis: this was asking great things of them.

But now with electrons and radio-activity and wireless telegraphy and all the rest, wonders in the ordinary sense of that word seem petty enough. That God made the world is less wonderful than that it made itself. That Christ died and rose and will return is less wonderful than all sorts of things we are believing about matter and its potentialities, and no more important.

What we want is not belief in mere facts that have happened—that this is so or that that has occurred. No one can get excited about such things in this age of wonders, of newspapers and the like. What we want is belief that so and so *shall* be so. Our creeds need to be thrown into the future tense. "We believe this will come to pass." What? A world of peace, a universal brotherhood, a genuine reign of God. Such a thing were never harder to believe than just now. Therefore we must believe it harder than ever. And no one can claim that this is an easy faith or lacks adventurous quality. Not some slight improvement in the social order but a world remade from top to bottom—that has the imaginative pull needed. About that we can say, Credo quia absurdum.

Faith as Jesus understood it was a power. If one had faith enough things would happen; the sick be cured, or mountains moved out of the way. But most of our creeds are wholly static. They deal with historic facts or eternal truths which remain quite the same whether we believe them or not. If we believe them as hard as we please, nothing happens. To Jesus faith mattered, and faith had power for it was belief in what was not yet but which, please God, should yet be.

That is the kind of faith we need, faith in the future. That is Christian faith and it is the only kind that is. Such faith puts us on our mettle. Such faith actually achieves things. Without it God can do little. With it he can do everything. The kingdom of God shall come, that is a faith that will work if we but get the world to believe it. And certainly no one can say that is an easy faith. Was there ever any faith harder?

Therefore we meet the challenge I quoted at the beginning, not with the Apostles' Creed or the Nicene Creed or the Thirty-Nine Articles or the Westminster Confession, but with the Lord's Prayer: Thy kingdom come. And on the faith that it will come we build our Christianity.

Section D

SOCIAL IMPLICATIONS

Chapter XXIII

PERSONAL RELIGION AND SOCIAL ETHICS

For some years past Christianity has been widely interpreted in terms of social service. The social gospel has been in control in many of our churches and we have witnessed a splendid flowering of social idealism and enthusiasm. But many are complaining that with it all there has gone a loss of vital religion—that devotion to one's neighbour has too often taken the place of devotion to God. Exponents of the social gospel have rightly replied that in serving their fellows they are serving God and showing their devotion to him. "Inasmuch as ye have done it unto one of the least of these my brethren, ye have done it unto me."

But when all is said and done, there still remains a lack. The social gospel has actually failed to meet certain legitimate needs—needs that are genuinely religious. It is time there was a revival of interest in religion as religion, and we may well be thankful for the signs that it is already upon us.

And yet this revival of personal religion is fraught with danger; the danger that the social enthusiasm and vision of our day may be dimmed, the progress toward better conditions be checked, and the gains already won be sacrificed. Evidently we are faced with a serious problem. A brief historical sketch will perhaps illustrate how serious it is.

To Jesus Christ religion was a profoundly personal thing. No one can read the gospels without realizing that he stood in a relation of closest intimacy with God, and that he drew from his communion with him inspiration, sustenance, and strength. On the other hand, in his ethical teaching he struck with emphasis the social note: "Whosoever would be great among you shall be your minister; and whosoever would be first among you shall be servant of all."

The apostle Paul was true to Jesus in his twofold emphasis on religion and ethics—personal religion: "Ye are not in the flesh but in the spirit, if so be the Spirit of God dwelleth in you"; and social ethics: "The whole law is fulfilled in one word, even in this, Thou shalt love thy neighbour as thyself." But already in Paul the tendency appears to emphasize personal morality—a tendency quite natural in the circumstances—and to make asceticism an element in the Christian ideal: "What concord hath Christ with Belial? Or what portion hath a believer with an unbeliever? And what agreement hath a temple of God with idols? For we are a temple of the living God. Wherefore come ye out from among them and be ye separate, saith the Lord, and touch no unclean thing."

After Paul the development went on apace, carrying the church ever farther away from the emphases of Jesus. For one thing religion was increasingly institutionalized. While it never wholly lost the personal note it became more and more a corporate and external affair, with rites and ceremonies and sacraments and public and formal worship. It is significant, for instance, that in the vast mass of the Christian literature of the second, third, and fourth centuries—of the period between John and Augustine—there is hardly a single passage of deep and vivid personal devotion. The language of religion, so far as it appears at all, is largely formal and stereotyped.

For another thing ethics was growing steadily more individualistic and self-centred. Asceticism was coming rapidly to the front and to be a Christian meant primarily to keep oneself unspotted from the world. According to the Epistle of James, "The friendship of the world is enmity with God." According to I John, "If any man love the world, the love of the Father is not in him."

The following picturesque passage from The Shepherd of Hermas, a Christian document of the early second century, well illustrates the common attitude: "As servants of God, you are living in a strange country, for your city is far from this city. If you know your city, in which you are going to dwell, why do you here prepare lands and costly establishments and buildings and vain dwellings? O foolish and double-hearted and wretched man, do you not understand that all these things are foreign to you, and are under the power of another? For the Lord of this city will say: 'I do not wish you to dwell in my city because you do not live according to my law.' If then you have fields and dwellings, and many other possessions, when you are cast out by him, what will you do with them? For the lord of this country justly says to you, 'Either live under my law or leave my country.' What then are you going to do? Will you, because of your fields and other possessions, deny your law, and walk in the law of this city? Take heed that this be not unprofitable to you, for if you wish to return to your own city, you will not be received. Beware then; as if living in a foreign country, gather nothing for yourself beyond your immediate needs, and be ready that, whenever the master of this city wishes to expel you for resisting his law, you may leave his city and depart for your own city, and joyfully follow your own law, suffering no harm."[1]

The resemblance to Bunyan's *Pilgrim's Progress* is striking. Christians fifteen centuries apart agreeing exactly in their picture of the Christian life! Not social service was the ideal of such men, but withdrawal from the world; not to save the world was their effort, but to escape from it.

In course of time this early tendency bore fruit in monasticism, the apotheosis of individualistic ethics. In monasticism morality as well as religion is read wholly in terms of man's relation to God, and his duty to his fellows drops out altogether.

In the great Father Augustine religion still has the personal note, as is abundantly shown by his *Confessions:* "Thou hast made us for thyself and our hearts are restless till they rest in thee." "Who will grant me

[1] Bk. III, chap. 1.

to find rest in thee? Who will grant me that thou mayst come into my heart and inebriate it that I may forget my ills and embrace thee, my only good? What art thou to me? What am I to thee that thou commandest me to love thee, and unless I do it thou art angry with me and threatenest great sorrows? Is it itself a small sorrow if I do not love thee? Ah, me. Tell me by thy pity, Lord my God, what thou art to me. Tell my soul 'I am thy salvation.' So speak that I may hear. Behold the ears of my heart are before thee, Lord; open them and tell my soul, 'I am thy salvation.' Hide not thy face from me. Let me die, lest I die, that I may see thy face."[2] This certainly is the language of genuine personal religion.

Yet it was the same Augustine who did more than any one else to establish the institutional and hierarchical theory of the Catholic church as the sole ark of salvation and the supreme authority on earth, and it is because of this that he is reverenced by the Roman Catholics as the greatest of the Fathers.

In Salvian of Marseilles, a younger contemporary of Augustine, we have a capital example of the way ethics could be made at once individualistic and ecclesiastical. In his tract on *Avarice* he says: "He who has done few good works has all the more need to make up for his neglect at the hour of death by giving to the church for the sake of the heavenly reward. He who has done many good works should do this also, for of good works there is never enough. He who has done

[2] Bk. I, chap. 5.

only evil ought at the end to seek his salvation by making the church his heir. He is not to think at all of his relatives and of those dependent on him, for it is necessary to care for one's self by seeking the salvation of one's own soul. What shall it profit a rich man to leave his son rich if he himself falls into hell? It is better for the children to be poor in this world than for the parents to be poor in the other."

With the passing of the centuries religion became increasingly institutional and ethics increasingly individualistic. To be sure there were frequent manifestations of personal religion of a very profound type. The literature of the Middle Ages contains many splendid expressions of it, as, for example, in the writings of St. Bernard; and now and then ethics broke loose from its bondage to personal salvation and became a genuinely social thing, as, for example, in the life and teaching of St. Francis of Assisi. But this was exceptional.

As a rule love was recognized simply as one virtue among many, having its place with the other virtues of the Christian life as a means of winning salvation, and so it found expression in charity rather than in the effort so to improve the conditions of life that charity becomes unnecessary. It is significant that Thomas à Kempis' *Imitation of Christ*, that beautiful book which has brought religious comfort and inspiration to multitudes of Christians, both Catholic and Protestant, contains no hint of social service.

It was Martin Luther's great distinction that he broke with the Catholic notion of religion and of ethics and returned to Jesus' estimate of both. Religion he interpreted as a genuinely personal thing: trust in God, making the Christian independent of institution and priesthood and sacraments. On the other hand he socialized ethics completely. No deed, he said, is a good deed if done for the sake of a reward: "Whoever turns good works to his own advantage does no good work." And again: "The highest art, the noblest life, the holiest conduct is the practice of love for God and one's neighbour." And what he meant by this is abundantly evident: "It is our neighbour needs our service," he exclaims in one of his sermons, "God in heaven needs it not."

But after Luther Protestantism fell back again into the old misunderstandings. Religion was not as generally depersonalized as in Catholicism, but ethics was as completely desocialized. This is seen perhaps most strikingly in Evangelicalism—the greatest revival of personal religion that Protestantism has witnessed. The ethical watchword of Evangelicalism was "Come ye out from among them and be ye separate." John Wesley, the great protagonist of the movement, declared, in characteristically trenchant phrase, that "Friendship with the world is spiritual adultery," and insisted that upon becoming a Christian you should cut loose from all your old companions lest you be corrupted by contact with them. What a contrast with the attitude of Jesus who was known as the friend of publicans and sinners! Happily, under the influence of the growing humanitarianism of the age, many of the Evangelicals were better than their theory and did much splendid service. But it was only secondary, not primary, and the net result of Evangelicalism, if it was to promote personal religion, was also to promote individualistic ethics.

In modern times, under various influences which I cannot stop to enumerate here, there has been an unparalleled development of social interest and effort; and the social gospel has taken almost complete possession of our more liberal and progressive churches. It is the great glory of our modern Christianity. But, as I said at the beginning, it has been accompanied by a decline in religion, and we may well rejoice in the current revival of religion.

But is this revival to mean the loss of the social gospel, of the splendid social enthusiasm of our day? God forbid! That were too high a price to pay. Better no religion at all than a religion that turns the attention of the best men—as much of the older piety did—away from the needs of earth to the glories of heaven and hinders the regeneration of this world in which we live. The substitution of selfishness, even religious selfishness, for the splendid altruism of our day would be no advance but the saddest kind of a retrogression.

How is it to be prevented? Not by socializing religion, as many seem to think. I have no quarrel, of course, with corporate and institutional religion, with public worship and the common expressions of the religious life of a church or community. On the contrary I recognize their great importance. When they are abandoned or neglected the religious life of the individual is apt to grow feeble and cold. But after all they are only the outer garment. At its heart religion is the relation of a man not with his fellows but with God. "Thou when thou prayest enter into thine inner chamber and having shut thy door, pray to thy Father who is in secret." If religion does not root itself in personal communion with the divine, public worship is apt to degenerate into mere mummery.

But this is an old difficulty and need not concern us here. It is another thing altogether that I am thinking of: the effort, very common in this modern age, so to interpret religion as to merge it wholly in the social gospel. Thus it has been interpreted, for instance, as the emotional accompaniment of social service, or the enthusiasm animating men's social ideals, or the confidence that our efforts will be crowned with success because in line with the divine purpose. Or, again, it has taken the form—as in the positivism of Auguste Comte —of the worship of humanity, the fields of ethics and religion being completely identified.

But this is to empty religion of its peculiar significance and to impoverish the life of man. For after all one's relations with one's fellows are not the whole of life, or should not be. The man who has no life of his own apart from the society in which he lives is a poor creature indeed. It is commonly said nowadays that personality is a social product, but unless it attain to some degree of independence over against the society which gave it birth it hardly deserves the name.

Religion is the greatest safeguard of personality the world has known. And in this age of feverish hurry and bustle and absorbing social enterprise personality particularly needs safeguarding. We are in danger today of becoming mere machines or mere cogs in a bigger machine, which means disaster not only to us, but to society as well; for if personality be impoverished, society suffers an irreparable loss.

In my opinion there never was so great a need of religion, of genuine personal religion, as there is now —of that consciousness of the invisible and the eternal which sets a man apart and makes him free. No man can serve the world as it needs serving unless he be in some measure independent of the world, with his life's roots struck deep in another soil.

I have said that we cannot meet the difficulties of the existing situation by socializing religion. Neither can we meet them by making ethics individualistic. This has been the great mistake in the past. Christians were so interested in personal salvation that they forgot their duty to society and mankind, and devoted themselves to the cultivation of their own personal virtues. Not that personal virtue is unimportant. God forbid! But unless it be made a part of a larger morality which embraces devotion to the good of others, it does not attain the level of Christian morality at all. Luther again put the matter in truly Christian fashion when he said: "The Christian does not live for himself alone in this mortal body, but also for all men on earth; and it is to this end he brings his body into subjection and labours and acquires property, that he may be able to serve others more sincerely and more freely."

The solution of our problem does not lie in making both religion and ethics personal, nor in making them both social, but in making the one personal and the other social. In other words, in seeing to it that personal religion bears fruit in the service of our fellows.

Jesus set the example for all his followers: oneness with God in the intimacy of personal communion, the service of man in the spirit of unselfish devotion. Personal religion becomes socially fruitful when we interpret the will of the God whom we worship in social terms, as we must interpret it if it be the Christian God we worship. Gaining sympathy with his ideals and becoming sensitive to his wishes, we give ourselves to the promotion of his good purpose—the reign of mutual sympathy and helpfulness and brotherliness here on earth. Thus interpreting God's will, we find religion and morality together in the most intimate possible fashion. They are very different from each other, but they are vitally one: love for God the root, love for man the fruit.

Or there is another way of looking at the matter. We may interpret love for man as an independent obligation, just as primary as the obligation to love God. As a matter of fact, in the ordinary course of human development love for others is even more original than love for God. It is in the society of our fellows we grow up, and it is they we are first conscious of. Normally indeed it is through knowing and loving them we come to know and love God. There is profound insight in the words of I John: "He that loveth not his brother whom he hath seen, cannot love God whom he hath not seen." It may fairly be said, I think, that to Jesus love of neighbours was just as primary as love of God. The truth is, Christianity involves not one obligation but two, equally imperative and mutually sustaining. If morality be the fruit of religion—the service of one's fellows growing out of the worship of God, religion is the fruit of morality—the worship of God growing out of the service of one's fellows. As Jesus put it, "If any man willeth to do his will, he shall know of the teaching, whether it *is* of God."

"Thou shalt love the Lord thy God with all thy heart and with all thy soul and with all thy mind. This is the first and great commandment. And the second is like unto it, Thou shalt love thy neighbour as thyself." It is not the whole of Christianity to love God. Nor is it the whole of Christianity to love your neighbour. Only the man who loves both God and neighbour, who lives in fellowship with the divine and gives himself in helpful service—only he has caught the true spirit of Jesus.

In view of all that has been said, I think we may in conclusion, without fear of misunderstanding, summarize the teaching of Jesus in the concise injunction: Personalize your religion; socialize your ethics.

CHAPTER XXIV

THE MINISTRY OF RECONCILIATION

In The Shepherd of Hermas occurs the following striking passage: "A revelation was made to me, brethren, while I slept, by a very beautiful young man who said to me 'Who do you think the old lady was from whom you received the little book?' 'The Sibyl,' I replied. 'You are wrong,' he said, 'it was not the Sibyl.' 'Who was it then?' I asked. 'The church,' he replied. 'Why then was she old?' I inquired. 'Because,' he said, 'the church was created before all things and for her sake the world itself was framed.' "[1]

This sentiment, which represents a common opinion of Hermas' Christian contemporaries, is shared, I take it, by few of us. In whatever ways we may be worse than the Fathers in this at least we have advanced beyond them, for happily we believe today that the church is not an end in itself, as the early Christians believed, but, like all other institutions, a means to a farther end. It exists to serve, we say, rather than to be served; to minister rather than to be ministered unto. Not the world for the sake of the church, but the church for the sake of the world, is the watchword, and justly so, at any rate for most modern Christians. How then can the church serve the world in the days in which we live?

[1] Bk. I, chap. 4.

The church has still the same work it has always had to do: to convert men from sin and selfishness to a new life of righteousness and service; to cultivate the sense of the presence of God and bring men into fellowship with him; to show them Jesus Christ and win them to glad and eager discipleship; to inspire them with a high and holy purpose and make them strong to conquer and achieve. All this the church has done and is still doing, to its everlasting credit be it said. All this indeed it will have to do in the future as in the past.

But the work of the church has not been confined to converting men and building them up in the Christian faith and life—central as this has always been and will continue to be. The church has had many other tasks to perform; tasks changing from time to time with the changing situation.

I wish to call attention to a task that is particularly pressing in our day, a task to which all the churches of Christ the wide world over ought to give themselves with all the consecration and wisdom they can command.

Back in the first century, almost at the beginning of its history, the Christian church was obliged to break with Judaism and assert its independence of the parent faith. Born within the family of Israel there was no sign at first that the gospel of Jesus meant a new religion and a new ecclesiastical institution, but gradually it became apparent that to confine it within the traditional bounds and make the observance of Jewish law and custom a precondition of Christian discipleship was to deny the very essence of Christianity, the free access of every human soul to God. And so the break had to come, resulting in permanent schism between Judaism and Christianity, and splitting the infant church itself into two mutually hostile sects. Schism is always an unhappy thing, and yet without this initial break, fraught with age-long enmity as it was, the Christian religion would not have been, and Jesus would have remained a mere Jewish prophet instead of the Saviour of the world. It was a big price to pay but Christians everywhere recognize that it was not too big. The church was right in freeing itself from its Jewish bonds at any cost.

Again in the sixteenth century Christians were faced with a similar task. Martin Luther did not intend to disrupt the holy Catholic church, of which he was a devout and loyal member. On the contrary he hoped that his gospel of the forgiving love of God in Christ and of a present salvation through faith alone would bear its legitimate fruit within the existing establishment. But he was doomed to disappointment, and when his gospel was rejected, and he, himself, excommunicated by the Catholic authorities, there was nothing left for him and his fellow Reformers to do but to build a new church independent of the old, and thus Western Europe was divided into two warring camps. Every one knows the countless evils that have sprung from this division, and yet again the division was justified. From it have come many precious gains that the modern world could ill spare: direct access to God without the mediation of church or priest, recognition of the dignity and worth of secular callings, assurance of salvation, making it possible for the saved man to give himself in disinterested devotion to the service of his fellows, and finally, religious liberty, which the Reformers themselves were little interested to promote, but which came inevitably as a result of the conflict of the sects. All this Protestants are thankful for, and they rejoice that the task facing the Reformers of the sixteenth century was performed so thoroughly, and that a vigorous and progressive, even though divided, Protestantism was the fruit of their efforts.

Once more, less than a century later, English Christians were faced with a similar task. If the Reformation is approved by fewer Christians than approved the early break with Judaism, still fewer regard with favour the break wrought by those humble and despised Separatists of the late sixteenth and early seventeenth centuries. The Anglican church felt itself justified in seceding from the church of Rome, but it could not look with equanimity upon secession from its own ranks. Those we call the Pilgrim Fathers first cut themselves off from the church of England and then from their native land for reasons that appealed to few of their contemporaries. When they insisted on worshipping God in other ways, required as they believed by his word, and when they denounced as tyrannical the civil and ecclesiastical authorities who compelled them to conform, they seemed only ignorant and narrow-minded literalists.

And when they condemned the State church and would have nothing to do with it because it contained multitudes of the unregenerate, they seemed only censorious and unpractical fanatics. And even their most loyal descendants are compelled to acknowledge that, for all their magnificent courage and faith and spirit of adventure, they were more bigoted, more interested in unimportant matters, and more insistent upon their own way than might be wished. Yet most of us are devoutly thankful for them and for the enduring foundations they laid in this western world.

Thus over and over again in the past the sacred task of Christians has been to assert one or another Christian principle at the cost of disunity and division. To regard schism as in all circumstances the worst of evils is to be blind to some of the plainest lessons of history. There are times when to stand apart and it may be alone is the most sacred of duties; times when any institution is best served by those who condemn and abandon it, when the world itself needs to be shaken out of its complacency by division and conflict, when nothing short of war will break up old evils and open the way for a new and better day. But there are also times of another sort when the great need of the hour is to harmonize differences and heal divisions; when Christians need to remind themselves that "Christ is our peace, who made both one and broke down the middle wall of partition." There are times, I say, when the great need of the hour is to harmonize differences and heal divisions, and this is such a time. The church of Christ, the great representative of the principle of human brotherhood, must give itself earnestly and prayerfully to the great task of reconciliation.

Let us examine the task. But first a preliminary word by way of caution.

The gradual emergence of free and independent personality is one of the greatest achievements of human history. The Calvinists of the sixteenth and seventeenth centuries, with their belief in divine sovereignty dwarfing all human authority, and modern liberals with their recognition of divine fatherhood endowing all men with the dignity of children of God, have done much to foster human freedom and independence. Such gains the world can ill afford to lose. All movements like imperialism, militarism, socialism or communism which tend to make men simply citizens of a state, parts of a machine, or members of a class are reactionary in their tendency. Formerly slavery meant the control of one man by another for the latter's profit. Now it commonly takes the form of control by a state or class. It is no less slavery because you are yourself a part of the larger whole. Such control may make for efficiency but at the cost of personality. Prussianism made Germany more powerful but Germany was less worthy of power because of the invasion of personality which Prussian discipline entailed.

It is not this kind of unity and harmony the world needs, but rather the association and co-operation of free and independent persons; not an autocracy, whether the autocracy be that of the individual or of the group, but a genuine democracy. This alone is in the line of human progress and this alone is truly Christian. We do not move forward when in the interest of unity or efficiency we substitute sameness for variety, the homogeneity of an undifferentiated mass for the heterogeneity of a society of free persons. If unity and efficiency can be had only at the expense of freedom, they will be bought too dear. But the experience of America in the War abundantly proved, if proof were needed, that 'ne sacrifice of free personality is not necessary, that a democracy can voluntarily discipline itself and 'chieve a degree and quality of efficiency not to be ar proached in an autocracy. The only thing needed is a task worth doing which can command the willing and glad allegiance of free men.

After this general word of c ution let us look at certain fields within which reconciliation is especially needed in our day.

First there is the reconciliation of the countless sects into which Christendom itself is divided. In a report published by the English Interdenominational Committee on the Army and Religion, and in the similar report of the American Committee on the War and the Religious Outlook, attention was repeatedly called to the soldiers' impatience with denominationalism; and on the mission field, as we know, the evils of our ecclesiastical divisions have been profoundly felt for some time past. Everywhere we are coming to recognize that in these divisions lies one of the gravest problems the church has to face, and yet they have had their place, and an important place, in the development of Christianity. They have often been the means of disclosing new worlds of religious experience, securing attention for hitherto unheeded aspects of truth, or safeguarding imperilled liberties. They have also been havens of refuge for the persecuted. It is difficult to see how without them the church could have weathered the storms of the last few generations; how Christians could have adjusted themselves to the changing conceptions of the modern world, were it not for the elasticity secured by sectarian variety. Many when persecuted in one church have fled to another and thus alone have been able to enjoy the privilege of continued Christian fellowship.

The fathers of our country did their work well. They laid the foundations of free churches in a free state and thus gave a chance for individuality in religious experience and belief to develop more freely and on a larger scale than ever before. This individuality is the glory of the churches of America. Let us never, because of eccentricities or because of unhappy jealousies and rivalries, forget the debt we owe to the many and diverse families of faith which have made America religiously the most interesting and the most vigorous country in the world. But it is not new sects we need now. The times have changed and the day has come for binding these separate and independent bodies more closely together. The most pressing duty of the church now is not to cultivate itself, but to lay hold upon the world and Christianize it.

The old individualistic interpretation of Christianity which made each man's own salvation his chief concern, comported, of course, with a completely divided church. Personal salvation may be found in any sect however segregated. But the task of Christianizing the world, of bringing Christian principles to bear upon it and making it over into the kingdom of God, demands the common effort of all Christian churches.

I must confess that I am not particularly interested in organic church unity; in the merging of all our churches into one great church. But so much unity—so much sympathy and friendliness and confidence and understanding—as shall enable churches to labour together for a common end, so much unity as shall lead them to sink their differences for the sake of co-operation in a common task—this I am profoundly interested in and this the age is demanding in no uncertain tones. The great reason for unity is the common task which can be achieved alone by common effort; the great hope of unity is the common task in doing which all thought of sect and self is forgotten.

This suggests another division in the ranks of Christians—the division between those who make the great end of Christianity personal salvation and those who make it the creation of a new social order. In many quarters this division is very sharp, and where it exists it weakens the church and limits its influence even more, I am inclined to think, than denominationalism itself. As a matter of fact it is largely due to mutual misunderstanding, as most of our differences are, and reconciliation ought not to be impossible. All intelligent and right-minded Christians, whether conservative or liberal, believe that Christian character is a thing of fundamental importance. Not even the extremest reactionary divorces personal salvation from personal character, and not even the most zealous prophet of the social gospel divorces social salvation from social character. The common note in both is character, and the difference is only in its interpretation.

Those are not altogether wrong who denounce our modern social gospel because it lacks the personal note, because it lacks, as is often said, spirituality. What they mean is that it looks too exclusively to institutions and neglects men, or that it looks too exclusively to their material welfare and neglects their characters. So far as they are amenable to this criticism exponents of the social gospel misinterpret Christianity as egregiously as those Evangelicals did who used to think of salvation as escape from punishment instead of escape from sin.

Those who emphasize the personal element are fundamentally right. But they are often wrong in interpreting the obligations of personality too narrowly. All Christians may well agree that a principal function of the church is to create and nourish Christian character if it be but recognized that Christian character is not something self-centred and self-absorbed but the service of humanity in the spirit of Jesus Christ. And to secure general recognition for this should not be difficult, for if those who are chiefly interested in the gospel of personal salvation do not feel obliged to lay all the stress on the personal and particularly the negative virtues in order to escape the danger of secularizing Christianity, they will freely admit that the social virtues are a part and indeed the major part of Christian character; for they, too, know that love for others was made fundamental by Jesus.

Our business then—the business of all our ministers and all our churches—is not to set the social gospel over against the gospel of personal salvation, or the latter over against the former, but so to interpret Christian character that the saved man will inevitably serve his day and generation in the spirit of Jesus Christ, and thus to unite all Christians in the common task of bringing in the kingdom.

Again there is crying need today for a reconciliation of certain classes of society which face each other in suspicion and distrust and threaten the economic stability of the world. Capital and labour, employer and employee, the captains of industry and the army of workers; in a well-ordered world certainly their interests ought to be identical, but in the chaos of our present age their interests are widely supposed to be antagonistic and mutually exclusive, and the result is hatred and war and revolution. The Christian church has no economic program to offer the world. It is not its business to assume the rôle of the economist, and those Christian preachers and teachers who attempt to do so only bring Christianity into discredit and weaken its power for good. But the church has a great work of reconciliation to perform in this sphere as well as in other spheres, and it is derelict to its duty if it does not do its best to help. It belongs to the church to preach the gospel of social service just as earnestly as personal purity and honesty; it is its duty to insist that all men shall live and work not only for their own good but for the good of the community as well, and that they shall not pursue their ends in such a way as to sacrifice the welfare of others to their own personal gain. Not that we should cease to think of ourselves and to work for ourselves and our dear ones—to expect or desire this is worse than folly—but that we should also work for larger ends and in common devotion to a larger good.

It is also the business of the church to teach persistently that all men are persons, not things, and that they must never be treated as mere tools. In our modern democracy we are learning this. Christianity taught it long ago, though its message was not always understood even by the church itself. It is the duty of the church to insist and keep on insisting that in all the relations of men with men and of classes with classes human personality shall be sacred and that its rights shall not be invaded for the sake of anybody's gain or power. The sacredness of human personality lies at the very heart of the Christian gospel. To proclaim it with such unanimity and with such emphasis that nobody can be ignorant of it or ignore it, is, I am inclined to think, the biggest service the church can render in the economic field.

Thus without assuming a rôle for which it is not fitted—without setting up economic programs and offering economic nostrums which it has no business to do—the church may spread a better spirit, may promote mutual understanding, and may contribute to the ultimate reconciliation of groups and classes that are now at war.

Similarly with the international situation that is engaging world-wide attention in these days and is causing so much anxiety. The tremendous growth of nationalism since the Middle Ages has resulted in a great enrichment of our modern civilization. Under its influence there have developed national traits and types of character of unquestionable value to the life of the world. Yet nationalism in all the centuries has been a breeder of war, and today it is widely recognized that it needs to be supplemented and held in check by some kind of internationalism.

One of the most pressing duties of the Christian church—which by its very nature is prophetic and creative—is to make internationalism a part of the Christian ideal and to enlist Christian devotion and consecration in its support. The internationalism I have in mind is not that of socialism, which means the spread of class consciousness and the extension of class war, nor ecclesiastical internationalism, which puts loyalty to church above loyalty to country, nor, indeed, any form of internationalism that undermines and destroys true patriotism. I have in mind rather an internationalism that heightens and enriches patriotism, as we strive to make our country strong and wholesome that it may better serve the world; an internationalism in which every nation, made just and generous by the patriotic devotion of its citizens, shall live righteously and brotherly with all the family of nations. Such an internationalism has never been made a part of the Christian ideal except by prophetic spirits here and there, but it must be. Divine revelation is progressive and we come only slowly into possession of the new truth God would teach us. One of the great lessons he is teaching in this age is that the Christian gospel applies just as truly to nations as to individuals. Let the church of Christ beware how it closes its eyes to this message! The church is an engine of untold moral and spiritual power. To get the backing of the Christian conscience for the right kind of internationalism will bring it within the range of possibility. Without that backing it will remain but a chimera.

What we need today, particularly here in America, is not to substitute internationalism for Americanism, but to reinterpret Americanism in such a way that it will involve international as well as national duties. It is a crying shame that in so many quarters Americanism spells selfishness instead of service. Americanism means labouring for a better America, but a better America means a country that is not only free and prosperous but whose freedom and prosperity are a blessing to the world.

It is not that our will is lacking but that our will needs guidance. The Christian devotion is here; the world indeed is full of it, and there is enough of it to transform completely our national relationships as well as our class-relationships in spite of all the skeptical and evil-minded in high places or low; but the devotion must be properly directed. Responsibility must be felt as keenly by the Christian church for teaching nations to dwell together in unity as for teaching Christian brothers to do so. And the church must courageously attack and expose all institutions and influences that make such unity more difficult. Unless an international conscience is developed in all parts of the world and into it is poured the consecration of religion, the world will go on floundering along generation after generation in the same old way, and war will follow war in the future as in the past. What the world needs is not a conscience that declares war wrong, but a conscience that leads men and nations so to live that war becomes unnecessary.

The church has many tasks in the present as in the past, but none is more pressing today than the task of reconciliation. Sects, parties, classes, nations: everywhere there is misunderstanding and estrangement. If there is any evil the gospel of Christ is meant to cure it is this. If it fails here no success elsewhere will atone for the failure.

Chapter XXV

RELIGION AND EDUCATION

It was a great thing for Christianity that in its early days it enlisted the support of educated men: Paul and the author of the Epistle to the Hebrews, the apostles of the second century, and the great Alexandrian Fathers, Clement and Origen, and countless others who were abreast of the best learning of their age. Had it not appealed to them and to others like them in every century, it would long ago have perished from the earth. History abundantly shows that no religion can permanently endure which does not secure the confidence and devotion of the educated classes of the community. An early and persistent rival of Christianity was the Persian religion of Mithra, which spread rapidly within the Roman Empire during the first two centuries of our era and attracted multitudes of adherents, particularly in the army. For a time it looked as if Mithraism might actually win the race and become the religion of the empire. But attractive as it was and impressive as were its rites and ceremonies, it had nothing for the intellectuals of the world—no profound philosophy, no great doctrines—and finally it perished before its small intellectual rival, Christianity.

Similarly in the latter part of the second century a Christian sect known as Montanism, closely akin in many respects to what we call pre-millenarianism, disputed for a position of pre-eminence within the church and threatened to sweep the Christian world. But it, too, was wanting in elements that could appeal to the thinking classes, and it faded out and disappeared.

On the other hand a religion that appeals only to the intellectuals is equally without elements of endurance. In the second century of our era, great thinkers known as Gnostics entered the Christian circle and attempted to transform the Christianity of the day into an imposing system of philosophy, denying the salvation and the salvability of any but the intellectually élite. It made a great commotion for a time, but soon succumbed to the pressure of a faith which disfranchised nobody, high or low, wise or unwise.

Similarly neo-Platonism, the most influential philosophy of the third and following centuries, essayed to be a religion and in the fourth century the Emperor Julian would fain have substituted it for the Christianity which he hated. But for all the depths and wisdom of its philosophy it had nothing for the common man, and while the influence of some of its ideas was permanent in Christendom, the movement itself survived but a few generations. "I am debtor both to the wise and the unwise" were the words of Paul, blazoned on his missionary banner, and because in every age it has had its message for both, Christianity still flourishes after nineteen centuries of growth.

While thus recognizing the necessity of the appeal to the untutored masses, as well as to the educated classes,

I am interested in this chapter particularly in the latter, in Christianity's adaptation to men and women of light and learning, to the cultured portion of the community, not simply to the college-bred, but to those who read and think and do most to determine the ideas and the aspirations of any age.

My first thesis, then, is that if Christianity is to appeal to such persons it needs the services of education. It captured the educated classes of the Roman Empire because it was put by Paul and other great thinkers of the early centuries, Clement and Origen of Alexandria, Ambrose of Milan, Augustine of Hippo, into the dominant forms of the age. In its cosmology and epistemology and ontology it spoke the language of the day, interpreting current ideas in the light of the gospel of Christ, and thus giving them a new significance. This Christian reinterpretation of the thinking of the Græco-Roman world was the work of centuries. It did not mean the abandonment of the categories and forms of thought and the vocabulary of the ancient world, but only the permeation of them with a new spirit and with new ideals. The result was a way of thinking, political, philosophical, social, and religious, in some respects profoundly different, in others to all intents and purposes identical with the old. This way of thinking remained for centuries almost unchanged. The Middle Ages deified the patristic age and strove to cast all its thought into patristic forms. Devotion to the Fathers was a passion, the infallibility of their doctrines was an axiom, and the defense and elucidation of their teachings were the chief occupation of the greatest European thinkers for many centuries. The Christian faith remained so long unquestioned because it was an integral part of the ancient heritage. Had it remained alien to the culture of the empire—a mere Jewish or Babylonian exotic in the Græco-Roman world—it would never have survived as it did. It was carried by the common stream that flowed from the ancient down through the mediæval world.

The break with the old, if I may change my figure, began in the fifteenth century and culminated in the eighteenth. The break was not primarily with Christianity, but with the old world of which Christianity was a part. Christianity suffered simply because it was so bound up with the old that it could not be or refused to be disentangled from it. It still exists largely in the old forms which were long ago discarded for almost everything except religion. Scientifically, economically, politically, socially, philosophically, we live in a new world, but religiously we still think in the old terms, and the result is a schism between Christianity and the intellectual classes of the day, which is very ominous for Christianity.

One great need of the present which should be keenly felt by all Christians of light and leading is to disentangle religion from the outworn forms of thought which belong to another age and make religion unpalatable or incomprehensible to multitudes of moderns. To show that religion is not identical with those forms of thought, that it is not a mere inheritance from the past, but is a spirit or an attitude which belongs equally in every age and may express itself in new world as well as old world ways of thinking; to reinterpret religion in modern terms for those who think in such terms, is one of the great functions of the religious thinkers of the present day. But is it not dangerous to read religion in such terms, to entangle it again with the forms of thought and the ways of looking at things that characterize the age in which we live? As time passes and other generations succeed our own, will not the thinking of the twentieth century become in its turn antiquated, and the religion which has been intimately bound up with it fall again into disrepute? Yes, the danger is very real. But two things should be said.

Religion cannot exist as a mere disembodied spirit any more than art or music can. Art cannot survive if there be no artistic productiveness, nor music if all use of instruments and voice be eschewed. Religion must express itself in emotions and ideas and activities, and if it is to be propagated and become the possession of many, it must clothe itself in beliefs and principles and institutions of one sort or another; if not in such as are congenial to the modern mind, then in those that are alien and outworn.

It should also be said that the danger is less serious than it once was, for the bondage of infallibility has been broken, it may fairly be hoped, forever. A principal difference between our own and earlier ages is that we do not attribute to the ideas of a present age, as the

Fathers did, the quality of absoluteness and finality. We do not expect our ways of thinking to endure forever, and we treat our reinterpretations and our formulations in the religious realm, as in every other realm, as tentative only and of temporary worth. Before our very eyes established theories in science, politics, and economics are undergoing radical change, and we are coming to realize that this is the normal order of existence. Ideas sit more loosely upon us than upon the Fathers, and as we hand them on to future generations, it will not be as chains for the human spirit, but as wings.

Yes, religion needs the service of education today as it needs it in all great creative epochs. Without its help the kernel cannot be separated from the husk; without its help the true spirit of religion cannot be made to speak in language comprehensible by the modern age. The outlook for religion, at any rate for Christianity, the only religion possible to most of us, seems dark indeed. But I do not myself think the outlook is dark, for I see disentanglement and reinterpretation going on all the time on an ever larger scale, and I firmly believe that religion will yet come to its own again in this modern world of ours.

I have been speaking of religion's need of education. Equally imperative is education's need of religion.

Religion is a major human interest and to ignore and neglect it is to leave education stunted and incomplete. Religion is as essential to a well-rounded liberal education as science or philosophy is. Much of the best in human thought and achievement has been motivated by religion, and without an understanding of religion is quite incomprehensible. The man who is not interested in religion and is without sympathy with it, is necessarily blind to the meaning of a great deal of the history of the past and the life of the present. He is guilty of provincialism, the one thing that a genuinely liberal education ought to make impossible. The evil effects of this sort of provincialism are seen in the modern economic interpretation of history with its assumption that men and women are controlled by economic motives only; an assumption that the Great War ought to have exploded once and for all, revealing as it did in clearer light than ever before that men are moved not simply by the desire for gain, but also by patriotism, by the passion for justice, by the love of liberty, by sympathy with the oppressed, in other words, by ideals all of them of the stuff of which religion is made.

If education is to be truly liberal, it must include the study of religion as well as of all the other major interests of humanity, not in order to make men religious —that is not the purpose of religious education any more than to make them artists or musicians or lawyers or doctors—but to give them an understanding of it and a sympathetic appreciation of its meaning and its influence.

The provincialism of an education which ignores religion is all the worse because as a rule it means in these days a tacit or avowed hostility to religion, a hostility easily explicable in view of the pretensions and intolerance of religion, but for all that ill-befitting a man of liberal culture and not permanently tolerable in an enlightened age. That the ignorant and uneducated should be prejudiced against those whose ideas and ways of doing things are alien to their own is only to be expected. We see such unenlightened prejudice exhibited on every side, particularly in these days against foreigners of all sorts. But such prejudice is always the work of an undisciplined or uninstructed mind and cannot permanently survive the white light of a genuinely liberal education. And this will in the end be true of the widespread prejudice against religion, which will go the way of the old prejudice against science. For after all religion is or should be a liberating, not an enchaining influence, giving a man larger outlooks and broader horizons. It is not religion against which hostility should be felt, but the abuse of it, the abuse of it due to the very ignorance and stupidity and narrow-mindedness which it is the function of education to overcome and destroy.

Again education needs religion because it profoundly needs idealism, and one of the greatest feeders of idealism is religion. Idealism indeed is itself a form of religion and cannot flourish where the temper and spirit are opposed to religion. In these modern days we have become so much interested in education for efficiency that we have largely lost the idealism which ought to preside over education, without which indeed no education can be a liberating and uplifting force. A sign of the widespread loss of idealism is the modern neglect of the humanities. There are many fountains of idealism—literature and philosophy and art—all these feed the human spirit and enable a man to commune with the prophets and dreamers of the past and make him conscious he is more than a brute. We are so concerned to train our children in expertness of eye and hand and brain that we forget that expertness is a good only when put to good ends. By all means let us cultivate all the powers, mental and physical, but let us also furnish these growing minds and bodies with the spirit that shall lead them to use their powers for worthy ends. To have one's capacities outrun one's ideals is a dreadful thing, even more dreadful when it is a nation and not merely an individual. One of the most ominous things about America has been the deplorable lack of idealism in high places in the State, among our own chosen leaders. Ominous it is not for America alone but for the world, and all the more ominous just because of America's tremendous resources and immense powers for good or evil. Where will the world be in the days to come and whither will it go without idealism?

Finally, education needs faith. The great reservoir of faith is religion. The faith we have in mind is not faith in this or that doctrine but faith in the possibility of achieving difficult things. A faith such as this is easy for children to entertain and for uneducated people, but difficult for educated men who have seen so many failures in human effort. Without faith, however, idealism comes to naught, remaining but an empty dream. Faith that the divinest force in the universe, that God himself is enlisted for high ideals is the g atest support of those very ideals.

Some think it dangerous to arouse such faith They fear it will turn men from earth to heaven an ead them to rely wholly on God. But this danger is chin -cal today. The modern man is bound to read his religi in terms of human betterment and to find faith in God not a substitute for but an incentive to human effort. Faith means faith in God not to do our task for us but to guarantee the divineness of our ideal. We believe in God not because we would have him do our work for us and bring a better world by miraculous power, but because we believe that, being divine, our ideal will gather to itself the devotion and the sacrifices of worshippers of God and lovers of their brethren and make them strong to conquer and achieve. Our hope and prayer is that all men and women of light and leading everywhere may have this idealism and this faith, so that human effort may be endowed with divine power.

Chapter XXVI

RELIGION AND A BETTER WORLD-SOCIETY

That everywhere men are thinking in world terms is a hopeful sign. It is a great thing, too, that the feeling of responsibility for a better world is also growing, for without such a sense of responsibility no improvement is possible. The task is rendered difficult, not merely by its immensity but by the fact that there is only one world and hence the spur of competition is lacking. There is required for the task, therefore, a new psychology and a new motive.

Our first question is, What do we mean by a better world-society? To three of its features I wish to call attention.

1. A world-society would be better than our present system insofar as it would be more idealistic. By idealism I mean a greater interest in the things of the spirit, in the things that differentiate us most from the brute. I mean an interest in and devotion to the things of the mind, to the cultural aspects of life, to the æsthetic, intellectual, and ethical interests.

Our modern material and mechanical development has largely absorbed us. Hence there is a peculiar need of idealism at the present time. To turn our eyes on other and more important things does not mean abandoning the material interests of life. They are not bad but good, unless too dearly bought. They mean a great advance in the march from mere animalism, but they are not enough. The spread of creature comforts alone will hardly satisfy the spirit of man.

The growing leisure of our time, increasing as industrialism makes the support of life easier, not only increases the opportunity for idealism but also makes such idealism imperative. Otherwise we shall fall back into animalism. There are two forms of animalism: constant physical toil, which makes men mere beasts of burden; and empty idleness, mere loafing or doing nothing. Many of the workers in our industries are no higher in civilization than the black folk in the tropics. Both are brutish. So there is an immense need of idealistic interests and occupations, intellectual and æsthetic, if we are to bring to pass a better world-society.

Our growing freedom also makes idealism increasingly important. The development of the race means greater freedom as maturity increases. Men move upward out of chattel slavery, out of economic slavery, out of political slavery. We may bind men by laws for a time; but compulsion must give way to spontaneous and voluntary activity. This cannot but happen as the masses rise in the scale of evolution. Slaves may be bound to decency by their masters; but free men must have the ideal of decency or they will wallow in indecency.

A better world means not simply better conduct but better men. Better conduct can be got by force and law but the world is not really better except where the better conduct is free and voluntary. We may need compulsion for a time, as in the case of children, but we cannot remain content with this.

All this means that idealism may not be the luxury of certain classes as in the past. Idealism is to be for all. Such a raising of the general level is very difficult to bring about, but with our modern means of communication it can be done. And it must be done or no better world will come.

2. A better world would be not only more idealistic but more brotherly. This means larger mutual understanding, sympathy, confidence, respect, good-will, and helpfulness. This means co-operative democracy. Suspicion must give way to confidence. Even good-will and helpfulness are not enough. We need an increase in respect, which will keep us from trying to force our ideals on others and violate their autonomy. Here it is difficult to draw the line, but draw it we must, for we shall not have a better world until prejudice and bigotry and pride are outgrown, as well as ill-will.

A lack of brotherliness is one of the gravest defects of the present age. Fortunately we are waking up to it, especially to the need of brotherhood between classes and nations, not simply between individuals. We have come to recognize that there is altogether too much international suspicion, fear, contempt, and ill-will. When communities and nations were isolated, local or national brotherliness was enough, but now this is no longer so. We must have brotherliness on a world-wide scale if we are to have a better world.

3. Idealism and brotherhood are not enough, however. A better world would be a more intelligent world. We must have intelligence to discriminate ideals and to know how to realize them and to make the spirit of brotherliness beneficial. Good-will without intelligence is particularly futile and often harmful. The lack of intelligence is perhaps the most notable defect in these recent days.

Our second question is, What is the place of religion in promoting a better world? What can religion do to help?

Let me remind you that religion is here anyway and let me assure you that it is here to stay, whether we believe in it or not and whether we like it or not. Religion is a natural instinct like sympathy, love or friendship. If one thinks it will disappear, it is because one thinks of a particular religion or form of religion. But religion is a major interest and is bound to have its will. It is not a question whether we shall have religion or not but whether it will be of such a sort as to help or hinder the coming of a better world-society. In itself religion is indifferent. Whether religion shall be a help or a hindrance is a question that non-religious people ought to be interested in as well as religious people.

Let us look at religion then in relation to the several elements of a better world-society of which I have been speaking: idealism, brotherliness, and intelligence.

1. To foster idealism is one of religion's principal functions. It turns men away from mere animal and

physical things to spiritual things, that is to say, to intellectual, æsthetic and ethical matters. It gives them higher interests and cultivates higher values. This religion has always done. It is the most idealistic force in history, the force that has done most to create ideals.

But religion has also often hindered the coming of a better world-society, or at least failed to help it. By its otherworldliness it has frequently made men indifferent to the present and so has been a bar to social progress. This is as true of Mohammedanism as of Christianity. Here the modern social gospel is the ground of hope. By its asceticism religion has frequently made men too indifferent to or contemptuous of physical things, such as health, comfort, and the like. One thinks of Hinduism and Christianity. Such an attitude is deplorable. Jesus was no ascetic and we are learning that the spiritual must be built upon the physical. A great ground for present hopefulness is the large development of the physical aspect of life.

If religion can avoid the pitfalls of otherworldliness and asceticism and nourish an idealism for the present world and for the whole man its opportunity to serve in promoting a better world-society is very great.

2. To foster human brotherhood is another of the principal functions of religion. This is Christianity's chief business. And it cannot be doubted that Christianity with its doctrine of the fatherhood of God and the brotherhood of man has done much to promote sympathy, confidence, respect, and good-will.

But religion has also hindered as well as helped

brotherhood by its sectarianism and bigotry. Religious men must strive to do away with them both. Much is in fact being done along two lines. Men are promoting church unity, or the spirit of unity; the thing itself in organized form is not necessary. They are also promoting friendliness between different faiths, Protestant and Catholic, Christian and Jewish, Mohammedan and the like. It is a great pity that all Christians are not doing as much in this way as are the liberals. Here in fact is the great opportunity of the missionaries: not to destroy other religions or to displace them with Christianity, but to enrich them with the best in Christianity and to enrich Christianity from them. And this is just what missionaries are increasingly doing.

Christianity's principle of brotherhood must also be enlarged to include not merely the fellow-members of a church or a class or a community or a nation but all the world. Jesus' general ideal of brotherhood, narrowed by Paul and John, needs to be recovered. Brotherhood must be interpreted in the sense of internationalism, not of a class but of whole peoples and all peoples. There is no limit to what religious men could do if they were to unite in making this their ideal. Without them it cannot be achieved.

3. To promote intelligence is, of course, chiefly the function of education, but religion has its place here, also. It has done much in the past in founding colleges and other schools. It should continue to promote and support education in every possible way.

But if religion is to help at this point it must stop

hindering the growth of intelligence as it is too widely doing. It has interfered with the advance of intelligence by its dogmatism. Religion has often set up beliefs which men must retain and beyond which they must not advance. This is fatuous and most harmful. Religion is free, like love and art, and dogmas are absurd. Dogmatism which prefers tradition to truth is as bad as patriotism which prefers the glorious to the true. Religion must outgrow the notion that it depends upon particular beliefs for its existence. In principle Christianity is not dogmatic.

Religion has also retarded the growth of intelligence by the whole notion of infallibility. Infallibility is as bad in religion as it is in science or anywhere else. It binds the mind. If religion is to promote the building of a better world it must abandon its dogmatism and its belief in infallibility and open the doors for the free development of the human spirit. Religion has sinned grievously and must repent.

The positive contribution of religion is the freedom it promotes, freedom in the largest sense. Religion should be above fear, full of confidence, afraid of nothing. Religion should not dwarf and narrow men but make them broader and bigger and freer. Rightly conceived it does just this. Wrongly conceived—as it too often is—it does just the opposite.

Religion, we may say in conclusion, has its place and its important place in building a better world. If it can but outgrow its exclusiveness, otherworldliness, asceticism, sectarianism, bigotry, dogmatism and obscurantism and can give itself consciously and deliberately to fostering idealism, promoting world-wide brotherhood and spreading the spirit of faith and confidence in God and man and truth, it can do much. If religion fails in its duty here it will go hard with the world. And if the world fails to avail itself of religion's help the better world will hardly come, for all the higher forces of our civilization must work together for betterment. And of these higher forces religion is certainly not the least.

Chapter XXVII

THE INFLUENCE OF THE CHURCH ON WORLD AFFAIRS

My subject is the influence of the church not upon personal character or upon the relations of individuals with individuals, or classes with classes, but upon the relations of peoples with peoples: the influence of the church upon international affairs.

And first let me refer to the influence of the church upon international affairs in other ages, to what the church in the past has done in this matter. In its beginnings the church was a small sect, set apart from the common life of the time, waiting for the speedy return of Christ and the end of the present world. In these circumstances the great virtue was unworldliness. Christians sought to live as much apart from the world as they could and to divorce themselves from its concerns. With the reform of the world and its improvement the church did not concern itself. This world was soon to pass away. To seek to better it seemed pointless.

When Christianity in the fourth century became the official religion of the Roman Empire, this conception of the Christian life and the Christian ideal persisted unchanged. The church had no new program for the new situation in which it found itself and it went on doing and striving for the same things as before. The only difference was that it now had peace and plenty. The only change was from persecution or tolerance to official recognition and prosperity as the state-religion. The monasticism of the period represented the continuation and organization of the same spirit that had controlled the church in the previous generations.

In the Middle Ages the western world was split up into warring tribes which were gradually consolidated into nations. The church, the only international institution of the western world, pledged as it was by its very principles to kindliness and mercy, did much to moderate the passions and to check the wars which would otherwise have been worse than they were. It condemned wars of aggression and exploitation and established the truce of God. It mediated national quarrels. To the church we must ascribe great credit for its moderating effect upon the antagonisms and rivalries of the time.

With the Protestant Reformation this international institution itself was broken in pieces and the spiritual unity of the nations was destroyed. Christianity in its Protestant form became a national instead of an international thing and religion tended to heighten and make more bitter the natural animosities between states. Only in modern times have we come to realize that it is the duty of Protestantism, since it has broken the old international ecclesiastical control, to supply something else and something better in its place. To supply this spirit and atmosphere of world-wide peace and brotherhood, I believe is the greatest function of the Christian church, whether Protestant or Catholic, indeed the great function of all religions in these days in which we live.

Let me then turn to the church of today, to its international duty and opportunity, to what it ought to do and can do for the betterment of international relations.

First of all, in my opinion, the church ought to do all it can to promote the closest possible relations among the nations of the earth. I do not mean political relations, international treaties and conventions, international associations or leagues or alliances. With them the church has nothing to do, for it is not a political organization and it has no place in politics. As an ecclesiastical historian, knowing what mischief has been wrought by the occasional incursions of the church into the fields of politics and what the church has suffered therefrom, I should be the last to want to see such experiments repeated. What I have in mind then is not political relations but human relations. To promote the closest possible human relations among the nations of the earth the church should do all it can.

Christianity believes in the brotherhood of man, not in the brotherhood of Americans or Englishmen or Frenchmen, not in the brotherhood of Protestants or Catholics, or even Christians, but of all men the wide world over as sons of a common Father. And one of Christianity's principal aims is to make that brotherhood an actual thing. One of its chief objections to war is that war interferes with such brotherhood and makes it impossible.

But the brotherhood of man, for which Christianity stands, is as inconsistent with isolation and segregation which many are urging nowadays as with war. It stands for intimate association among peoples, without which there can be no brotherhood. In other words, brotherhood involves a world-fellowship, a world-wide fellowship. Even if world peace were to be had by isolation—and in these modern days of course it cannot be had thus, for nations are so tangled up together that they cannot be disentangled by anything short of destroying the railroads, the steamboats, the telegraph, and the radio—Christianity could not approve it; for isolation limits human brotherhood and confines it within bounds which Christianity cannot tolerate. A Christianity that remains national and declines to look beyond the borders of its own nation is no genuine Christianity. It denies the very fundamentals of its faith. As Paul put it, "God hath made of one blood all nations of men to dwell on all the face of the earth."

Peace therefore by isolation the church cannot approve, even if it were feasible. The church must transcend national borders, by foreign missions, by charity to the suffering and the starving, by helpfulness in all sorts of ways to peoples the wide world over. Christian interest in human welfare and Christian helpfulness cannot stop short of human need wherever it may be. The slogan, "Am I my brother's keeper?" were words of Cain and the church repudiates them. Christianity insists that we have no right to shirk our obligations to our brethren. What this may involve in political treaties or associations the church does not pretend to say, but it insists upon the spirit of brotherhood and will be content with no legislation that denies or flouts it.

Again the church must do all in its power to do away with hatred and suspicion and distrust among the nations. Much of this spirit is manufactured for selfish or sensational purposes, much of it is due to ignorance. The church has a direct interest in the press and ought to denounce the use of the press to foment international suspicion and hatred with the same vigour with which it denounces sins of impurity and dishonesty. Education is needed here and the church should interest itself in and insist upon such education as shall overcome national hatred and suspicion. It should denounce slander and misunderstanding. By this I do not mean that only good should be said of other people but that with them as with us evil is exceptional and not the rule.

The church ought also to promote active good-will. This is what love for one's neighbour means, of which the Old Testament and the New have much to say; not personal affection but active good-will. It should make the promotion of international kindliness and good-will as much a part of its teaching as personal kindliness to one's immediate neighbour. The kind of nationalism that means the glorification of the nation (America, Germany, etc.) at the expense of other nations or the love of one's country by hatred of other countries should be everywhere denounced for the unchristian thing it is.

Only as international hatred and distrust disappear and active good-will prevails among the nations and peoples of the earth can world peace, the great and immediate need of the age, be established and maintained. The church has a very important, indeed an indispensable part to play in the establishment and maintenance of world peace. Without its support and backing all efforts in the direction of world peace will fail of their aim. The proper work of the church is in the realm of the spirit, not in the realm of things; to affect attitudes, to influence men's hearts, to promote the spirit and temper of peace; to create an atmosphere of peace without which all treaties must break down.

Yet the atmosphere of peace alone is not enough. Even if all the peoples of the earth desired peace it could not be maintained without agencies for the settlement of disputes and the clearing up of difficulties. With such agencies the church has nothing to do, but with the spirit which those agencies exist to give expression to the church has everything to do. If agencies of peace are set up while the spirit of war prevails among the people they will be thrown aside or transformed into instruments of war.

But the absence of hatred and distrust and suspicion among the nations and the presence of mutual good-will are not enough. The human brotherhood for which Christianity stands demands co-operation among the nations, just as it demands it among individuals. Mutual helpfulness is not enough. Work for common ends is necessary. Only as these common ends seem important enough to lead to the subordination of differences can we have permanent peace. Co-operation in the Great

War for a common end kept the allies at peace among themselves but now that the war is over other ends must be found or they will fall out again. Individual and separate self-interest are not enough. It is just as likely in certain emergencies to lead to war as to peace. But there are some common ends big enough to bring about co-operation.

Material things are limited in amount and the more one nation has the less there is for others. The earth doubtless is fitted to support all that now live upon it or may live upon it, but it cannot supply unlimited superabundance of material things. If wealth, overwhelming military and naval power, vast material resources be the supreme ambition of all, war will result again as always.

But if human ambition be set on the arts and sciences, on wisdom and philosophy, on virtue and generosity, justice and peace; and if men learn to be content with enough of the physical goods to keep them well and comfortable, world peace is permanently possible. But not otherwise. So the church should make more earnest than ever with its message, Seek ye first the kingdom of God. It should teach its people to appreciate spiritual values at more nearly their true worth. It should show that all material possessions are but means to higher ends, to render genuine human living possible, for human life is distinguished from that of brutes just by its intellectual and spiritual qualities.

If the relations among nations I have been referring to are to be promoted an immense amount of such idealism is necessary. To cultivate idealism in the peoples of the earth is one of the principal functions of religion, whether Christianity, Judaism or any other. And this is the great need of the age. However the ideals of Christianity may be phrased—whether collectively as the kingdom of God, or severally as purity, honesty, justice and the like—they constitute the very meat and drink of the Christian church in all the ages. From the beginning down to the present day the church has been the teacher and champion of ideals as over against selfish and material ends. And it has always sought to arouse faith in the possibility of realizing them. If the first curse of our day is selfishness, the second is skepticism. Christianity is a constant protest against faintheartedness. At its centre is the doctrine of the new birth. It stands for the achievement of things men count miracles. Its question is not whether the goal be possible but whether it be desirable. Faith is the conviction of the possibility of accomplishing the seemingly impossible.

To continue in ever greater measure to supply spiritual ideals—the arts and sciences, philosophy and culture—which alone are fitted to be ends for international co-operation, is the church's greatest international duty and opportunity.

Chapter XXVIII

THE KINGDOM OF GOD

The present age is notably religious. I will not say that there is more religion within the Christian church than in other days, or that we Christians are distinguished above our fathers by the sincerity and vigour of our religious life, but certainly the many religious sects that are springing up all about us, the growing discontent with existing forms of faith, and the eagerness of many both within and without the established religious communities to listen to those who have anything new to offer in religious lines, are an evidence of a deep and wide stirring of religious impulse and interest. Humanity at large is so constituted that religion of some sort may fairly be regarded as permanently necessary to it, but as the needs of men change the religions in which they have been trained may easily cease to meet their new demands, and a new faith may come to be substituted for the old. This has occurred repeatedly in history. The displacement of the Greek and Roman paganism by Christianity is one of the most notable and familiar instances. Christianity won its victory in the Roman Empire and became finally the religion of the state simply because it met the needs of the age as the older religions were unable to do. The faiths of Greece and Rome were the fruit of ancient conditions, and even before Christianity appeared new needs had developed which made new religious ideas and practices a necessity. The result was that foreign cults of all sorts became popular, and the old ones underwent large changes in the effort, conscious or unconscious, to meet the new situation. Had Christianity not come upon the scene the traditional paganism, radically modified to meet the demands of the day, might have retained a permanent hold upon the Roman Empire. But the new faith, born in the new age, and responsive from the beginning to its new needs, was fitted as the older could not be to become the religion of the new world, and its victory was inevitable.

It has often been remarked that our age bears a striking resemblance to the period in which Christianity first saw the light. The eager curiosity, the social unrest, the lively intercourse between different parts of the world, the developing spirit of cosmopolitanism and sense of human brotherhood, the disappearance of old and familiar landmarks, the common questioning of traditional standards, the multiplying of religious sects, the prevalence both of rationalism and of superstition, the loss of faith and the search for certainty—in all these and many other respects there is a close kinship between the earliest and the latest of the Christian centuries. It was a period of change on a vast scale and so is this. Are we to suppose then that as the ancient paganism gave way before the young and lusty Christianity so Christianity in its turn is to be crowded off the field by some new faith? There are those who seem to think so, and who talk about Christianity as an outworn system fitted only for an age that is gone. In reply to them it is not enough to show that Christianity still meets many needs of many hearts, needs which remain very much the same, that it comforts the sorrowing, strengthens the weak, raises the fallen as it has always done. It must be shown rather that Christianity not only does this but also meets the new needs of the new age.

What then is this new age? What are its characteristic features and its peculiar needs?

The modern age is marked by a vast confidence in the powers of man. For many centuries it was the custom to think of man as a weak and puny thing. Humility and self-distrust were the cardinal virtues, pride and self-reliance and independence the root of all vice. The change is not the fruit of speculation, a mere philosophical theory as to man's relation to the universe, but the result of the actual and growing conquest of the world in which we live. We are not completely its masters, to be sure, but we understand it far better and control it far more effectively than our fathers did. The past century has given the most brilliant demonstration the world has ever seen of what human power can actually accomplish in the material realm, the realm of the tangible and the visible and the audible. Science and mechanics have combined to give the modern man a sense of mastery undreamed of in other ages. What this man most needs, and he is the representative man of the modern age whose presence in overwhelming numbers chiefly distinguishes this age from those that have preceded it—what this man most needs from

Christianity is not condemnation for the pride of accomplishment, exhortations to humility and the offer of healing from above, but the chance to use his strength in ways that are most worth while—higher ideals, larger opportunities, vaster realms of service.

Another marked characteristic of the modern age is its widespread and controlling interest in the present world. With all its sorrow and suffering and distress, the world seems to the representative modern man a better and a more beautiful and a more satisfying place than it did to the representative man of an older day. It is not simply that this earth has become more interesting as we have learned more about it and the present life more comfortable as material conditions have been improved, but that the future possibilities of human life upon this planet seem so tremendous. Characteristic of a former time was its conviction that all had been learned and accomplished that man was capable of, that the golden age lay in the past and that nothing better was to be looked for. Characteristic of the present time is its faith in the future, based upon its solid experience of the past.

And again, what the age needs from Christianity is not a demonstration that this earth is a poor and unsatisfying place, and an exhortation to set one's heart upon another life beyond the grave but the vision of a work worth doing now and here, a work worth doing for this world, in which the thought and interest of the modern age so largely centre.

Another characteristic of our age is its growing social concern, which is the fruit in part of the modern interest in the present life just referred to, in part of the general emphasis on solidarity and unity which succeeded the eighteenth-century emphasis on individuality. The social conscience of Europe and America is now more wide awake and more generally active than ever before. Opportunities for social service are steadily multiplying, character is more and more interpreted in social terms, and their obligation to labour for the promotion of the welfare of society is increasingly felt both by individuals and by institutions. Our generation is burning with zeal for social, economic, and civic reform, and is controlled by the idea of human brotherhood and marked by its practice as no generation ever was before.

And again, what such an age needs from Christianity is not to be told the supreme importance of personal salvation but to be given a social ideal grand enough to fire its imagination, to arouse its enthusiasm and to enlist its devotion.

Has Christianity then a message for the modern world? Let us see. The greatest fact in modern Christian history is the rediscovery of Jesus. He is better known and understood today than he has ever been before. The development of historical study and criticism, which has revolutionized traditional opinion upon all sorts of matters, has given us a new insight into the origin and growth of Christianity. The Jesus of the Gospels has been finally set free from the integuments in which the devotion and the misunderstanding of the

Christian church early enswathed him, and has been allowed for the first time to speak for himself. And the
striking feature of the situation is that he speaks a language which the modern age, with its genial confidence
in man, its vivid interest in the present world and its
profound concern for social betterment, is peculiarly
fitted to understand. His message is just the message
that the modern world is looking for. The kingdom of
God was the burden of his preaching, not a kingdom
lying in another world beyond the skies but established
here and now—"Thy kingdom come, Thy will be done
in earth"; not a kingdom made up of isolated human
lives moving along their several and separate paths toward heaven, but of the society of all humankind band-
ed together in common labour under the control of a
common purpose. And not by some supernatural and
miraculous means was the kingdom to come while men
sat by and gazed in awe upon the power of the Almighty, but by the work of Jesus himself and of those that
came after him, by the devotion and energy of human
lives working at one with the Divine Will. When
Jesus said "Follow me" he meant nothing else than labouring with him at the same task in the same spirit.

The kingdom of God on earth, what does it mean?
We answer perhaps glibly enough: the control of the
lives of men and of all their relationships one with another and of all the institutions in which those relationships find expression by the spirit of Jesus Christ
who has shown us what God is and what he would have
this world be. The answer is tremendous in its sweep

but it needs to be given a more definite content. What is actually involved in the kingdom of God on earth? Is it only a vague form of words, a beautiful but intangible mirage, or is it really something concrete and practical? Does it affect only ethics and religion, or social, economic, and civic matters as well? Does it mean only the improvement of individual character, or also the transformation of society and the state? The modification of details in our existing systems, or their radical reconstruction? The grafting of new principles on the old, or the repudiation of all we have and the birth of a new world? Can our present civilization really be Christianized, or must it give way to an altogether different order? Is it a dangerous thing, this kingdom of God? Does it cut too deep to be welcome, or is it simply the fulfillment of our faith and hope? And how is the kingdom to be established? What methods are to be adopted, what principles followed and along what lines must the work proceed? It is not to answer them that I have propounded such momentous questions as these. Who indeed can answer them today? It is only to emphasize the vastness and complexity of the problem. In it the church of the twentieth century, to which has been committed the responsibility of leadership, has the most difficult problem it has to face. We Protestants have hardly more than played with it hitherto. In the Middle Ages the Catholics grappled with it, and actually evolved an international state which they called the kingdom of God and which dominated western Europe for centuries. It was a grand conception, magnificently carried out, but it was not the kind of kingdom Jesus was thinking of, nor the kind of kingdom the world needs today. We live in the modern age and the modern age has turned its back forever on mediævalism, whether in state or church. We do not want the spirit of otherworldliness to distract men from their duty to this world but to inspire them to it; we do not want the future to overshadow the present but to transfigure it; we do not want the supernatural to crowd out the natural but to fill it with living meaning; we do not want a recrudescence of priestly or ecclesiastical authority but the birth of the spirit of Christian service. Freedom, spontaneity, individuality, opportunity, confidence, and self-reliance—all these precious gains of the modern age we must preserve. But we must have also love, sympathy, fellowship, co-operation and an ideal worthy of our common devotion, our common effort and our common sacrifice.

The kingdom for which mediæval Christians toiled so faithfully was for still another reason quite a different thing from the kingdom of God which Jesus had in mind. He did not mean another institution set up in the midst of the existing institutions of the world into which a man could enter from without. The kingdom of God which he preached is not in any sense identical with the Christian church. It is the reign of God, of his purposes, of his ideals, of his spirit in the relationships and in the institutions of the world. It is the world itself brought into harmony with God's will. Not a dualism of two kingdoms but one kingdom only, God's world and ours controlled by the spirit of Christ. For this the Christian church is called to labour, not to enlarge and glorify itself and to seek to dominate but to make itself the most efficient instrument for the transformation of the world into the kingdom of God.

It is a vast and splendid thing, this kingdom of God of which Jesus dreamed. It is not for one type of mind, one form of character, one sort of temperament alone but for all the sons of God the wide world over. It is rich enough to supply the most varied needs. It offers opportunity to the strong, activity to the strenuous, visions to the seer, comfort to the sorrowing, peace to the troubled, to all service in doing or enduring, in giving or receiving in the spirit of Christ, in active conflict or in quiet meditation.

It is a divine thing, this kingdom of God. In it God's supreme purpose finds expression, his purpose to promote the reign of the spirit of love among men. It is for this that God is; and this is what God's love for the world means. In human brotherhood the Divine Fatherhood finds fulfillment. Through human brotherhood alone the Father's purpose for his children comes to accomplishment, and through human brotherhood alone his children discover him. God himself is back of the kingdom. We did not invent it. Its ideals are not of our making. They have been given us. They are higher than we could have dreamed of. They lift us above ourselves. We rise to meet them and find expressed in them the best that we can know. In this kingdom the divine and the human are inextricably interwoven. In it there is communion with God, as his desires fill our souls and his purposes are made our own, and in it there is the power of God, as the inspirations of his presence lay hold upon us. And yet it realizes itself only in the experience of men. We do not find it by turning our backs upon the world and ceasing to be human, we find it only here in human life itself. It is rooted in the inner man, in his affections, his will, his character, but it comes to visible expression in all sorts of ways, as the external relationships of life are brought one after another under the control of the inner disposition.

It is both material and spiritual, this kingdom of God. It ministers to the body and to the soul. Not as in earlier days when the church thought only of the spirit and looked upon the body with contempt; not as today so many social reformers—even Christian ones— seem to think only of the body and disregard altogether the higher things of the spirit. Unlike both, Jesus ministered at once to the outer and the inner man. The kingdom of God which he proclaimed means the weal of the one as of the other. It means a social order in which there shall be food and drink and clothing and shelter, a just share of the physical goods of life for all God's children, and in which there shall be also for all of them the consolations of divine communion, the inspirations of human fellowship, the glow of sympathy, the joy of service, the trinity of faith and hope and love.

It is a Christian thing, this kingdom of God. The greatest gift of God to the world is Jesus Christ. It is just this which differentiates the kingdom of God we preach from all man-made Utopias. His life, his character, his teaching, his work, his spirit of service dominating the world—this is what the kingdom means. It is not merely our self-taught love and devotion but the love and devotion of the Christ kindled in our hearts as we have looked upon him and caught the inspiration of his vision of God. The prophets too preached the kingdom of God, but they had not seen Jesus; and it is not the kingdom of the prophets we proclaim to the world but the kingdom of the Christ. In him God has given the full revelation of his purpose for the world, and his aims, his motives, his estimate of values, his hopes it is that we would have the world share.

It is a uniting, not a dividing force, this kingdom of God. Not setting the present over against the past, the church over against the world, the conservative over against the radical, one community, one nation, one sect over against another. It gathers them all up into one. For it is broad enough to include all the best of the past and of the present and of the future yet to come; grand enough to enlist the devotion of men of every people, clime, and faith; and large enough to unite the whole world in a vast confederation of labour, not for the greatest good of the greatest number but for the greatest good of all; a kingdom which brings with it good for everybody and evil for nobody; not the good of competition which blesses one at the expense of another but the good of co-operation which blesses both alike. Not by jealousy and envy, not by sectarian zeal and religious fanaticism, not by national bigotry and class prejudice, not by the forcing of opinions and customs upon others but by the union of all men of good-will of every race and religion and condition, by the sharing of their visions and by the linking of their faiths and hopes and efforts shall the kingdom of God come.

The great task of the Christian church of the twentieth century is ready to its hand. Upon the church devolves the chief responsibility for the bringing of the kingdom, for to it has been vouchsafed the supreme vision, in Jesus' revelation of his Father's will. The church has had many large tasks in the past which it has met in a spirit of consecrated heroism—the conversion of the Roman Empire, the planting of a Christian civilization among the barbarian peoples of western Europe, the establishment of the world church of the Middle Ages, the recovery of the gospel of Christ and its incarnation in new institutions in the sixteenth century. It is in the face of great tasks that the church has always shown itself at its best, and it may well be grateful when they come. If ever there was such a task it is before us now.

We are on the eve of great happenings. No one familiar with history and able to read the signs of the times can for a moment doubt it. Unfortunately the church, as too often in the past, has in many places lost its leadership. It continues to minister beautifully and efficiently to its own members and to bless the lives of multitudes of them, but it is not in the van of progress, and much of the best life of the world has turned its back upon it and is pushing on alone.

We Christians are apt to be much too easily satisfied. We are complacent if our churches hold their own, if our better families can still be counted on, if respectability still dictates, even though hardly so imperatively as in other days, connection with the church and attendance upon its services. But this is not to be in command of the situation, and it gives no large promise for the future. We are content with too little, and the great modern world, with its teeming masses, its eager enthusiasms, its burning problems and its untold possibilities, is in danger of slipping away from us. Yet what a message we have for it! The kingdom of God on earth—the control of all the relationships of life and of all the institutions of society by the spirit of Jesus Christ.

Is it a mere idle dream—the coming of God's kingdom in this our world? It is the dream of Jesus himself, and shall not his disciples share his faith? Is it vain, after all the efforts of these nineteen centuries, to hope that the thing can ever be done? But the thing has never been really tried. That is a momentous fact to be taken account of in every estimate of the future. The Christian church has tried to do all sorts of things and in many of them has been eminently successful. But it has not made the kingdom of God on earth—which is the spirit of brotherhood, the reign of the spirit of Christ in all the relationships of life—its one supreme aim. So we need not be discouraged because the work is still unaccomplished.

Made wise by all the experiences of the past, endowed with a new charity and breadth of vision, taught the evils of disunion and the necessity of co-operation with all the forces of goodness everywhere, the church is justified in facing its mission with renewed courage and confidence. Let us no longer stand on the defensive. Let us no longer regret a past forever gone; let us no longer be content to minister to the needs only of a small portion of the community; let us no longer indeed think so much about needs, and think more about responsibilities and opportunities; and let us keep our eyes fixed upon Jesus' glorious vision of the kingdom of God, of a new earth in which dwelleth righteousness, of a regenerated world controlled by his spirit. So will Christianity again, as in the days of its youth, rise exultant to a world-wide task. This strong, manly, eager, busy age will respond with enthusiasm to an ideal worthy of its best effort—the transformation of this great earth into the kingdom of God, Christ's Father and ours.

NOTES

Page 3. Chapter I. What Is the Christian Religion?

The first two paragraphs of this address appeared in an article entitled "Christianity in the Light of Its History," in *The Hibbert Journal,* vol. XI, 1913, pp. 726 *ff.* Part of a brief introductory paragraph from Chapter XXIV is also to be found in *The Hibbert Journal,* vol. XIX, 1920, p. 123. Doctor L. P. Jacks, the editor, has given his permission to publish these extracts here. The remainder of this paper, as well as all the other material included in this book has, so far as can be discovered, never before been published. This address is also one of the few which cannot be dated. The subject was not the author's choice. He accepted it as it was assigned him and interpreted it to mean: What light does the history of Christianity in its whole course throw upon the nature of the Christian religion?

Page 16. *Section B.* Christianity Old and New.

These four chapters are a series of lectures which Doctor McGiffert was invited to give at the Auburn Theological Seminary in 1924–25. Owing to illness he was unable to deliver them. After his resignation from the presidency of Union Theological Seminary he decided to publish them as a small book; and with this end in view made a number of revisions of the original manuscript. When he came to write his *History of Christian Thought,* however, he incorporated some of the material of the first (and longest) lecture in the chapters on "Jesus and His Disciples," "The Apostle Paul," and "Irenæus." These portions have been omitted from the present chapter on "Primitive Christianity." For an account of Jewish Christianity and its central belief in the Messiahship

of Jesus, see McGiffert, *A History of Christian Thought,*
vol. 1, pp. 9–14.

Page 107. Chapter VI. Christ an Element in Christian
Theology.

This is the substance of an address delivered at a theological
conference in Union Theological Seminary in May, 1909.
Widely separated in time as are the six chapters in this section on Jesus, they exhibit a point of view that remains essentially unchanged.

Page 114. Chapter VII. The Lordship of Jesus.

The precise occasion and date of this address at Union Theological Seminary are unascertainable. It was probably used at
the commencement exercises in 1907, as an address to the
graduating class.

Page 129. Chapter VIII. Saved by His Life.

This is the substance of an address given at Union Theological Seminary Chapel, April, 1924.

Page 132. Chapter IX. The Living Christ.

This was delivered at Cornell University, April, 1924, and
at Union Theological Seminary Chapel.

Page 142. Chapter X. The Unsearchable Riches of Christ.

This is the substance of an informal talk given at Morning
Prayers at Union Theological Seminary in December, 1919.

Page 145. Chapter XI. What Makes a Christian?

The date and occasion of this discourse could not be ascer-
tained.

Page 151. Chapter XII. God and Human Need.

This address was delivered as a sermon at the First Church
in Plymouth, Massachusetts, in August, 1921.

Page 164. Chapter XIII. Christian Theism.

This paper was read at a meeting of the American Theological Society in April, 1922; and also at a Student-Faculty Conference of Union Theological Seminary.

Page 175. Chapter XIV. Communion with God.

This brief and informal outline was written in 1903 to be read privately to a small group of Union alumni who were among Professor McGiffert's choice students. It was never written out in full for formal publication, although it has in recent years been more widely circulated. It was from this unpublished paper that Doctor Ambrose White Vernon quoted in his Memorial Address, "Arthur Cushman McGiffert, 1861–1933, Scholar and Historian," in Union Theological Seminary Chapel, May, 1933.

Page 187. Chapter XV. The Christian Freeman.

This address was delivered at a union meeting of churches in Salem, Massachusetts, in November, 1921.

Page 201. Chapter XVI. The Christian Temper.

An informal chapel talk given at Morning Prayers at Union Theological Seminary in November, 1920, is here presented in substance.

Page 203. Chapter XVII. Forgiveness.

A Faculty and Student Conference at Union Theological Seminary in April, 1923, was the occasion of this address.

Page 209. Chapter XVIII. The Second Mile.

This is the substance of an address given at Mt. Holyoke College in March, 1917, and at the Presbyterian Church in Rensselaerville, New York, the same year.

Page 212. Chapter XIX. The Sense of Proportion.

Doctor McGiffert delivered this address at Wellesley College in January, 1920, and at Union Theological Seminary Chapel and the First Presbyterian Church of Englewood, New Jersey, the same year.

Page 223. Chapter XX. The Place of the Sacraments in Protestantism.

This is one of many papers Doctor McGiffert read at *Chi Alpha* in New York City. He became a member of this century-old clerical club in 1894. The date of this discussion is 1908.

Page 232. Chapter XXI. Vision.

First used in 1915 as a sermon at the installation of a graduate of Union Theological Seminary, this was also given in Montclair, New Jersey, in 1920.

Page 240. Chapter XXII. Credo Quia Absurdum.

This is the outline of an informal talk at Morning Prayers at Union Theological Seminary Chapel, December, 1923.

Page 245. Chapter XXIII. Personal Religion and Social Ethics.

This address was delivered at the Central Presbyterian Church and the Community Church of New York City, as well as at Union Theological Seminary Chapel, in 1924.

Page 257. Chapter XXIV. The Ministry of Reconciliation.

An address given at the Broadway Tabernacle, New York City, February, 1923.

Page 272. Chapter XXV. Religion and Education.

In 1922 this was delivered at Mt. Holyoke College and at Union Theological Seminary; and more informally at the Faculty Club of Hamilton College.

Page 282. Chapter XXVI. Religion and a Better World-Society.

As one of a series in a course given by several men this is the substance of an address delivered at Columbia University Chapel, July, 1923.

Page 290. Chapter XXVII. The Influence of the Church on World Affairs.

Doctor McGiffert was asked to speak on this subject by the Men's Brotherhood of the First Presbyterian Church of York, Pennsylvania, in 1922.

Page 298. Chapter XXVIII. The Kingdom of God.

This address was delivered several times, at the Madison Avenue Presbyterian Church, New York City, the White Plains Presbyterian Church and in Brooklyn, in 1909. It has been selected as the final chapter of the book because it presents a thesis and a phraseology dear to the author's heart.

INDEX

Agnosticism, 11, 100.
Amalric of Bena, 10.
Ambrose, 274.
Apostles, 37, 40, 65.
Apostles' Creed, 27, 114, 125, 145, 242.
Arminians, 68.
Art, 84, 276, 280, 296.
Asceticism, 19, 58, 69 ff., 83 f., 92, 190 f., 246 f., 286, 288.
Atonement, 89, 109, 173.
Augustine, 4, 37, 39, 58, 164, 223, 227, 247 ff., 274.
Authority, 65, 97 f., 101; of Bible, 97; of church, 37 ff., 74, 97; of Jesus, 7.

Baptism, 18, 60, 225.
Baptists, 231.
Barnabas, Epistle of, 26.
Benedict of Nursia, 4.
Bernard, St., 3, 250.
Bible, 7, 12, 19 ff., 39, 63 f., 73, 78, 97, 99 ff., 116, 145, 232.
Boniface, 4.
Brotherhood of man, 124, 127, 192, 236, 262, 284 f., 292 ff., 295, 299, 302, 306.
Brown, W. A., 85 n.
Bruno, Giordano, 10.
Buddhism, 6, 8, 148.
Bunyan, 248.

Callixtus, 33.
Calvin, 70, 226 f.
Calvinism, 68, 71 n., 206, 262.
Capital, and labour, 135, 191, 267.
Catholicism, Roman, 7, 32 ff., 69 ff., 83, 130, 223, 304.
Celsus, 21.
Channing, 13.
Chiliasts, 24 f.
Christianity, 3 ff., 18, 31 ff., 45 ff., 49, 76, 86, 142, 145, 147, 156, 203, 210 f., 238, 272 ff., 291, 298 ff., ethical religion, 8 ff., 21, 68, 228 ff.; Jewish, 17.

Christology, 22, 107 ff. *See also* Jesus Christ.
Church, 4, 12, 31 ff., 74, 120, 158 f., 257 ff., 270, 290 ff., 304 f., 309 ff.; Anglican, 230, 260; Calvinistic, 62; Greek Catholic, 33 f., 66; Lutheran, 62, 230; Roman Catholic, 55 f., 60, 66, 77, 223, 230, 249; in politics, 267, 269, 292.
Clement of Alexandria, 3, 164, 272, 274.
Clement of Rome, 23, 25, 27, 32.
Clifford, W. K., 210.
Communism, 262.
Comte, Auguste, 253.
Confucianism, 7 f.
Creed, 74, 77, 124, 240. *See also* Apostles' Creed, Nicene Creed.
Cyprian, 4, 33, 43, 66, 223.

Death, 17, 34, 90, 93, 108, 130, 141, 153, 197.
Deism, 89, 133, 145, 156, 164.
Democracy, 50, 220, 236, 263, 268, 284.
Dickinson, G. L., 156.
Disciples, Jewish, 11, 18, 20, 56, 138.
Dualism, 5 f., 19, 27, 73, 92, 109 f., 119, 134, 164.

Education, 217, 272 ff., 287, 294.
Edwards, Jonathan, 10, 172.
Epicurus, 133.
Erasmus, 57 f., 96.
Eriugena, John Scotus, 3.
Ethics, 8, 74, 214 ff., 225, 246 ff. *See also* Ideals.
Eucharist, 18, 60. *See also* Lord's Supper.
Evangelicalism, 11, 93, 130, 142, 251 f., 266.
Evolution, 42, 80, 283.

Faith, 61 f., 136, 145, 160 ff., 197, 201, 210, 240 ff., 280, 297.
Fear, 64, 81, 108, 196, 235 f.
Fénelon, 3.

319

UNION THEO. SEMINARY
LIBRARY
NEW YORK

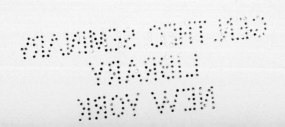